0.5X (Camera)

Beginners Guide to

iPHONE

11 SERIES

FOR THE ELDERLY

Tips, Tricks & Hidden Features Manual to Master Your iPhone 11, 11 Pro and 11 Max As a Senior

CHARLES

SMITH

Copyright

Printed in the United States of America
© 2019 by Charles Smith

Churchgate Publishing House
USA | UK | Canada

Contents

3

4

5

Who Needs This Book?

You just bought the iPhone 11 or 11 Pro, and haven't learned anything new on the device? Or you have been searching for some advanced tips and tricks to enable you to master this device? Or you are an Android Switcher or Novice iPhone User looking for a guide to help you navigate through the iPhone? Then this Manual is for you. It is time to dig in to see what settings and features you can tweak to get the most out of your iPhone 11. This manual will guide you through basic to advanced features and also enhance your ownership of the iPhone 11, 11 Pro or 11 Pro Max. It also presents some hidden tips and tricks that you never knew could be done on the device.

About the Author

 Charles Smith is a tech enthusiast with over 13 years of experience in the ICT industry. He is a geek and passionately follows the latest technical and technological trends. His strength lies in figuring out the solution to complex tech problems. Charles holds a Bachelor and a Master's Degree in Computer Science and Information Communication Technology respectively from the MIT, Boston, Massachusetts.

Dedicated to all Tech Geeks

1

Introduction

Apple released three iPhones in the iPhones 11 Series – The iPhone 11, iPhone 11 Pro and the iPhone 11 Pro Max. Apple focused on four major things for the new iPhone – the design, display, battery life and Cameras. The iPhone 11 Pro looks almost exactly like the iPhone XS from the front, although it is a little bit heavier and thicker. Except you are comparing them directly, you probably won't notice the difference in weight. You get a much bigger battery in exchange for that extra size which leads to a four hours battery life increase on a regular pro and a five-hour jump for the Pro Max. However, the big difference from the iPhone XS is at the back of the phones. The rear glass for the iPhone 11 Series is now stronger and it comes in a frosted matt finish which does not pick up fingerprints. It also integrates a glossy Camera bump with three Cameras.

On the contrary, the iPhone 11 has only two cameras. Images taken from the iPhone 11 series has far more improvement to that of the iPhone X. This improved picture quality is due to what Apple called Semantic Rendering. The Smart HDR recognizes what is in the image and renders it appropriately. This is how it works; firstly, the iPhone starts taking photos to buffer up the instance you open the camera App. By the time you press the camera button, it captures four underexposed frames of the photo, then it grabs one over-exposed frame. This is basically what also happens in the iPhone X, but the difference is that the iPhone X does not capture theoverexposed frame.

Secondly, Smart HDR and Semantic Rendering looks for things in the photos it recognizes e.g., faces, hair, the sky, etc. Then it uses additional details from the underexposed and overexposed frames to selectively process the areas of the images it recognizes. Hairs get sharpened; the sky gets de-noised, faces gets retightened to make them look even. Smart HDR is also less aggressive in flattening the photos, and sha-dows are corrected to regain detail. Finally, the whole image is saved, and you have a photo. These all happens instantly every time you take a photo, which is a testament to how powerful the iPhone 11's processor is. The iPhone 11 is powered by an A13 Bionic Proce-ssor which is a far improvement of the iPhone X's A12 Bionic Processor in terms of Processing speed. There is also a new chip in the iPhone 11 called the U1, which does precise positi-oning using an ultra-wideband radio.

The Standard iPhone 11 and the Pro Version Which Should I get?

It is a tough choice to make when planning to purchase any of the iPhone 11 series. The iPhone 11 Pro Starts at $999 with 64GB of storage, and the 11 Pro Max starts at $1099. The Pro Max cost $1449 for the 512GB storage version. The Standard iPhone 11 offers almost everything you get from the pro for $699, and you still get the improved wide and ultra-wide cameras, the front ultra-wide lens, the A13 Bionic processor, etc. The extra money on the pro buys you a superior display, a telephoto camera, and improved LTE performance.

Physical Features

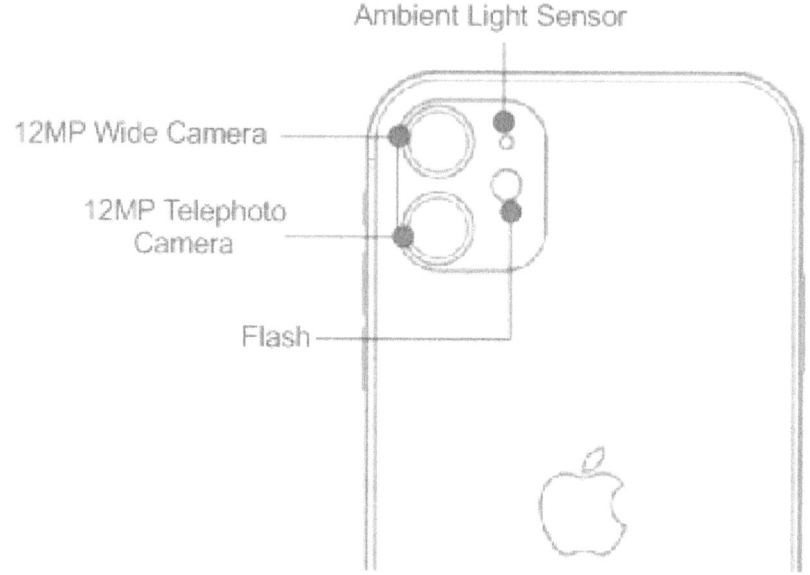

Rear View of iPhone 11

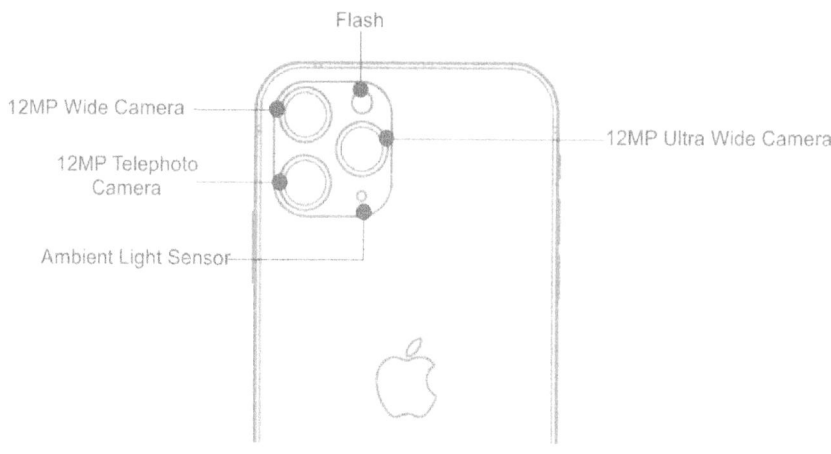

Rear View of iPhone 11 Pro/11 Pro Max

The Display

The display of the iPhone 11 pro is the new OLED Super Retina XDR display. It runs from the top to the bottom with a notch at the top, rounded corners and uniform bezels. The significant upgrades on the screen are around brightness and power efficiency. The screen is now brighter than previous version of the iPhone and uses 50% less power. The color processing of the screen is so natural with Apple's tone system turned ON.

The Side Button

The side button of the iPhone 11 is at the top right-hand side of the phone. It is the most used button on the phones and the recommended grip on the phone is such that the index finger of your left hand easily rests over the side button. This makes for easy pressing of the button using the index finger of your left hand.

Volume Button

The volume buttons include the volume up at the top and volume down buttons below. The volume buttons is used in combination with other buttons for other functions besides increasing or decreasing sounds. Holding down the Volume down button for several seconds activates silent mode in the iPhone 11 and 11 Pro. Other functions of the volume buttons will be described later in the manual.

Rear Facing Cameras

At the back of the iPhone 11 Pro are three rear cameras and a flash. We have the wide, ultra-wide and telephoto cameras. The telephoto camera has the same basic sensor as that of the iPhone X but with a faster 52MM/F3.0 lens. The Wide Camera has the same F/1.8 lens and a slightly better sensor, while the New Ultra Wide Camera is twice as wide as the Wide Camera with an F/2.4 lens. There is a clear distinction between the standard lens and the telephoto lens of the iPhone 11 cameras. The telephoto lens has two functions (1) to zoom in optically two times (2X) without losing the image quality. (2) to take portrait photos. The portrait mode allows you to have a sharp and crystal clear focus on the primary subject and everything around the subject blurs out into a creamy background. This is known as Boca effect. With the Secondary Camera, you have five different modes to play around with – studio light, control light, stage light and Stage light monochrome.

You can select any of the three cameras to take photographs or record videos. The front-facing camera is also updated to record 4k videos at 24, 30 and 60 frames per second. Cameras on the iPhone 11 series have augmented reality improvements for objects with the ARKits technology. What this does is better detection of Objects in front and behind on the camera's frame. There is also a new audio zoom feature that matches audio with the framing of your video, zooming in the videos and the sound generated by the object being recorded.

The flashlight also saw some improvements on the iPhone 11. It is now 36% brighter than that of the iPhone X, XR and X Max.

Speakers

The crystal-clear speakers of the iPhone 11 Pro are found underneath the phone and sounds louder than ever with Spatial Audio. It produces a new improved audio quality that supports Dolby Atmos.

Microphone

The microphone is also positioned underneath the phone.

Lightning Port

This is found underneath the phone. It is where the lightning cable is plugged into and the cable is connected to a lightning adapter to charge the phone.

Front Speaker

At the front above the screen is a speaker to receive voice calls.

Front Facing Camera

By the side of the front speaker is a 12MP front-facing Camera with an f/2.2 lens for taking wider-angle selfies and it also serves as

Face ID scanner. There is also a sensor which emits a purplish light by the side of the front camera. The reason you see this light blinking is because Face ID sends out some infrared lights emitted through the sensor which is picked up by the front camera.

Additional Accessories of the iPhone 11 Series

Several accessories come in the box your iPhone 11. They include; 18 Watts USB-C wall adaptor brick, Apple Ear-pod, lightening-to-3.5 mm jack adaptor

18 Watts USB-C Fast Charger

This allows you to plug the phone directly into your wall socket. Before you plug it into a power source, connect the USB end of the charging cable to the wall adaptor and plug the other end of the lightning connector cable into your phone lightning port.

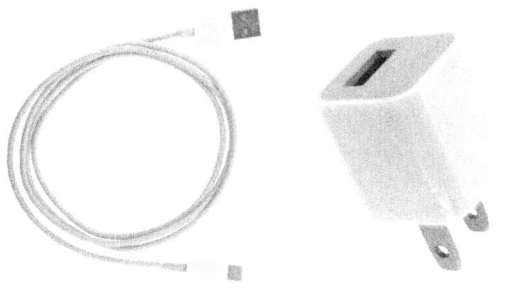

18 Watts USB-C Fast Charger and Cable

When the wall adaptor with the charging cable is plugged into the wall socket, it charges your iPhone.

Apple EarPod

The Apple EarPod is used for listening to music and receiving calls on the iPhone. The Apple EarPods are labeled R and L – which stands for Right and Left respectively - indicating the side of the ear the pod should be attached. The other end of the Apple EarPod has a lightning connector which is plugged into the lightning port beneath the iPhone.

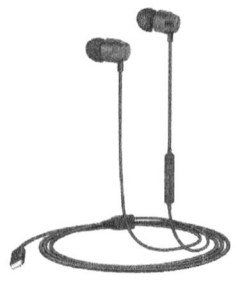

Apple EarPod

One thing to quickly note is the control area on the EarPod. This control area has a built-in microphone, volume up and down. Which means you can take calls from your EarPod as well as control the volume of sounds that go through it. The center button on the control area is used to play or pause music. Pressing and holding the center button also activates Siri. We will get into how to interact with Siri in details later on in the manual.

The Apple EarPod is an accessory to the iPhone 11 series. However, the AirPod does not come in the box; it is sold separately for $159.

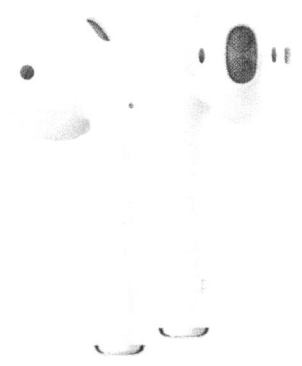

Apple AirPods

Lightning-to-3.5mm jack adaptor

This allows you to plug the lightning connector into the iPhone's lightning connector port and then use any set of headphones that has 3.5mm jack with your iPhone.

Lightning-to-3.5mm Jack Adaptor

2

Setting Up Your iPhone

Inserting SIM

The iPhone 11 series (11, 11 Pro and 11 Pro Max) require a SIM to set it up. Insert the SIM card tool into the SIM card tray opening at the right side of the iPhone and gently pull out the SIM card tray. Insert the SIM in the tray and gently push it into the phone.

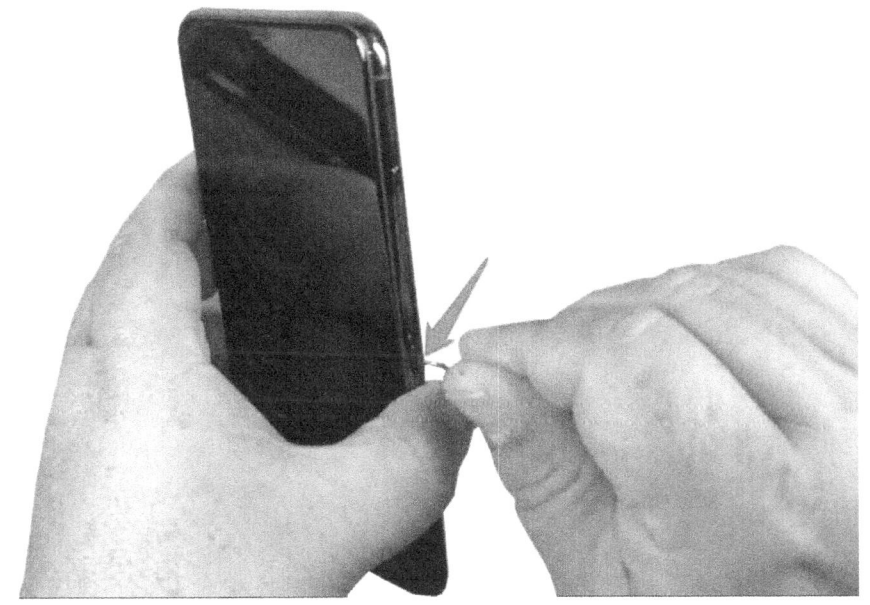

After inserting your SIM, Power ON the Phone and follow the prompts to set it up.

English   >

简体中文   >

繁體中文   >

日本語   >

Español   >

Français   >

Deutsch   >

Русский   >

Português   >

Italiano   >

First, select your Language > Scroll down and select "ENGLISH." Next, select your COUNTRY > e.g., "United States." Yours may be different. If you have an old iPhone, it is easier to select the

"Quick Start" option, else select the option to "Set up Manually."

Quick Start

If you have an iPhone or iPad running iOS 11 or later, bring it nearby to sign in automatically.

If you want, you can also set up this iPhone manually.

Set Up Manually

To use the "Quick Start" option, bring the old iPhone with all your information > on the old iPhone, tap on "Unlock to Continue" button on the "Setup iPhone New iPhone" dialogue box. > enter your passcode and tap on the "Continue" button > hold the camera of the old iPhone over the iPhone 11 to scan the code on the screen.

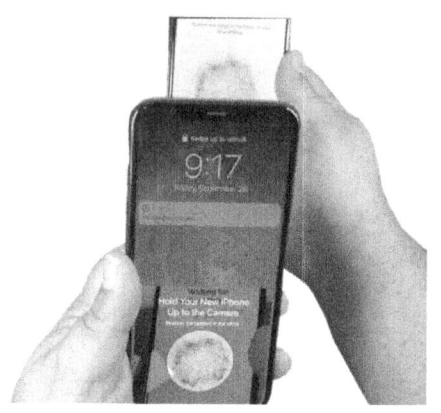

The transfer of information from the old iPhone to the iPhone 11 starts immediately after the scan is successful. This will take a couple of minutes, depending on the size of the transferred file.

Face ID

Prompt for Face ID setup process pops up on the screen after the transfer of the files from the old iPhone to the iPhone 11 is completed.

Face ID

iPhone can recognize the unique, three-dimensional features of your face to unlock automatically, use Apple Pay, and make purchases from the iTunes and App Stores.

About Face ID & Privacy...

Continue

Set Up Later in Settings

The Face ID is an improved security feature of the iPhone. It uses your face to unlock your iPhone and perform other bio-metric and security functions. You can either set up the Face ID during the set-up process by taping on the "Continue" button or choose to set it up later by taping on "Set up Later in Settings." We will look at how to setup Face ID later in the manual. So we will skip face ID setup for now.

Apps & Data

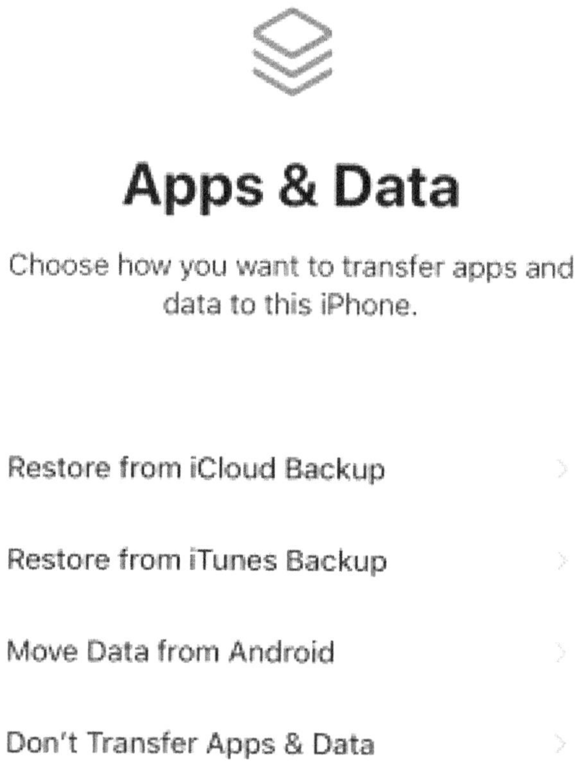

Apps & Data

Choose how you want to transfer apps and data to this iPhone.

Restore from iCloud Backup   >

Restore from iTunes Backup   >

Move Data from Android   >

Don't Transfer Apps & Data   >

"Apps & Data" is the next step in set up process. You are asked to either transfer data from an old iPhone or tap on "Other options" to restore them from your iCloud backup, from mac or PC, or move Data from Android. If you have iPhone data backed up on your iCloud account, you can transfer them to your new iPhone. You can also move data from an Android device into your iOS 13 powered iPhone 11, 11 Pro and 11 Pro Max. Keep in mind that to transfer data from an Android device to your iPhone 11, they have to be on the same Wi-Fi network. Tap on "Don't transfer Apps & Data" to skip this step.

We will look at the steps to backup and transfer data from the iCloud in details later on in the manual.

Keep Your iPhone Up to Date

**Keep Your iPhone
Up to Date**

Get the latest features, security, and
improvements by updating iOS
automatically.

You will receive a notification before
updates are installed, and can choose
other options in Settings.

Continue

Install Updates Manually

Next, you are prompted to "Keep Your iPhone Up to Date." Tap "Continue" to keep your iPhone up to Date during the setup process or tap on "Install Updates Manually" to do this later on. Steps to keep your iPhone Up to Date

will be discussed in details later on in the manual.

Apple Pay

Next in the setup process is Apple Pay. Apple
Pay allows you to add a debit or credit card to
your Apple wallet to make seamless purchases
on the Apple stores or any other stores. You

can skip this step during set up and do it directly in the wallet later. Tap on "Set up later in Wallet."

iPhone Analytics

iPhone Analytics

To help Apple improve its products and services, pre-release versions of iOS automatically send diagnostics and usage data. This can be changed in Privacy settings. Diagnostic data may include location.

About Analytics & Privacy

Next stop is the iPhone Analytics setup page. iPhone Analytics enables users to share data with Apple about their iPhone's performance, you can tap on the "Share with Apple" button otherwise, click on "Don't share" to protect your privacy.

Display Zoom

Display zoom setup allows you to choose how you would like to view your iPhone. There are two options to select from - ZOOMED and STANDARD. Selecting the ZOOMED option presents a larger text and controls while, the STANDARD option fits more icons and apps on the screen. The Standard display option is the recommended option. This choice can be changed at any time via the settings menu. Tap on "Continue" to move to the next option. You will get some basic instructions on how to navigate through the iPhone; click on the "Continue" button until you arrive at the "Welcome to iPhone" window.

Some Quick Tips

Power ON & OFF Your Phone

The steps to turn ON/OFF your iPhone as well as carry out an emergency restart if it freezes is what we will look at here. The easiest way to turn ON your phone if it is in a sleep mode is to press the side button once. When the phone turns ON, Face ID scans your face, then swipe up from the bottom to access your phone Apps Menu. You can also tap on the screen to wake the phone up. The phone is sent to sleep mode by pressing the side button again. This process doesn't completely power OFF your phone.

To completely power OFF your iPhone 11, press the power button and the Volume down buttons simultaneously until the "power to slide Off option" appears on the screen. This brings up three sliders – <u>Medical ID</u>, <u>Emergency SOS</u> and <u>Power OFF slider.</u> What we are interested in here is the "slide to power OFF." Slide it to power OFF your phone completely. We will talk about the Emergency SOS in details in subsequent chapters. It is vital to completely power OFF your phone at least once every month to refresh your phone and prevent it from slowing down.

If the phone is completely turned OFF, you can turn it back ON by pressing and holding the side button. It pops up with the Apple logo. You may need to input your passcode to access the app menu.

Force Resetting Your Phone

You could encounter a situation where the iPhone freezes while in the middle of an activity. The only way out of such a situation is to force reset the phone. This is done by pressing and holding the VOLUME UP, VOLUME DOWN and the SIDE buttons simultaneously for 10 seconds and this will force reset your phone. This completely shuts down the phone without the need to swipe. Another method to do this is to press and quickly release the volume up button, press and quickly release the volume down button and then press and hold the side button until you see the Apple logo. You should only use forced reset when you encounter a glitch while operating your phone and you can't power OFF the phone the default way.

iPhone 11 Gestures

Tap

Briefly touch surface
with the finger tips

Double Tap

Rapidly touch surface
twice with finger tips

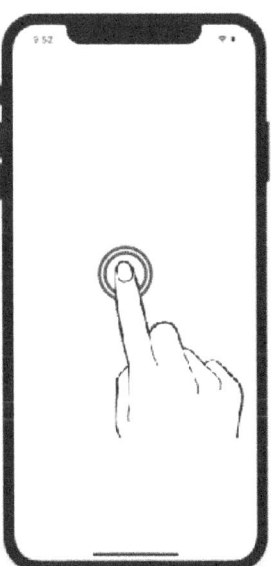

Haptic Touch

Formerly referred to as 3D touch, Haptic touch is touching the surface for an extended period of time

Drag

Move finger tip over surface without losing contact.

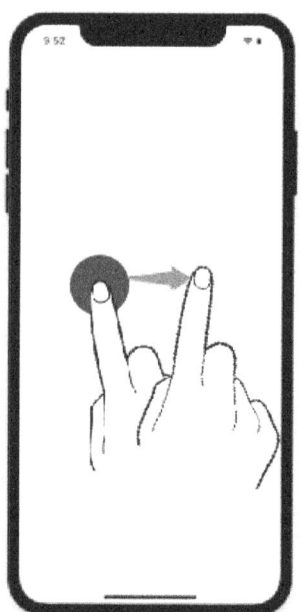

Pinch

Touch surface with two
or three fingers and
bring them close
together

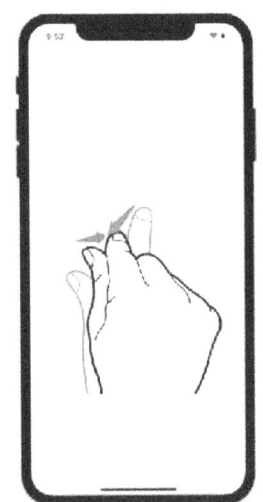

Spread

Touch surface with two
or three fingers and
move them apart

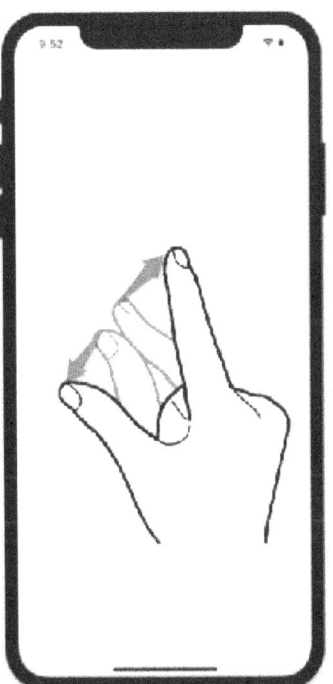

Swipe Up

Move finger tip over
surface from bottom-up

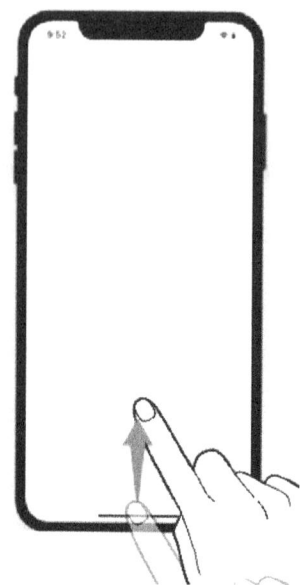

Swipe Down

Move finger tip over
surface from top-down

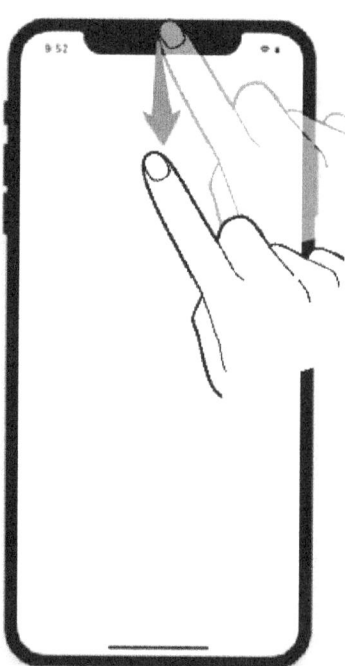

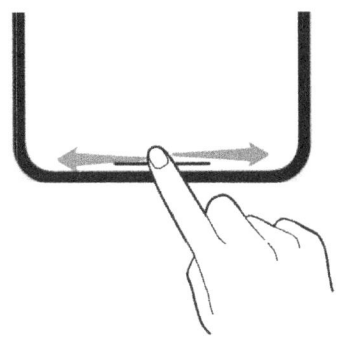

Move Finger tip on the surface to either left or right.

Basic Navigation

If you are a first time user of an iPhone, you need to know how to navigate through the iPhone 11 series.

Opening and Closing an App

Once you wake up your phone by pressing the side button, or using Face ID, you can access an App by swiping up to reveal the App menu. Click on the app you wish to open. To exit the apps, swipe up from the bottom and it closes the App.

Switching Between Applications

If you are in an application, but you wish to switch to another opened application at the background; from the current app, swipe from the bottom up slowly and let go. You get a card view from where you can switch left or right to different apps. Use the bar below each opened app. Another way to switch between apps is to hold the "horizontal bar" at the bottom of the app and swipe over left or right and it goes to the next application.

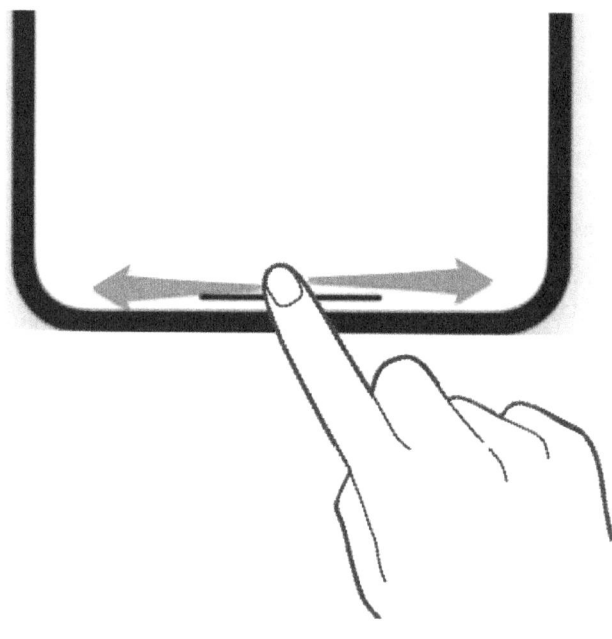

Swipe back and forth between applications using the simple bar right at the bottom.

Finding and Opening App Quickly

If you are looking to find and open app relatively quickly, or to close other apps you might have at the background, swipe up from the bottom edge of the screen and pause. This might take a couple of tries to perfect. This then takes you to a multitasking window where you can see the different applications that is open.

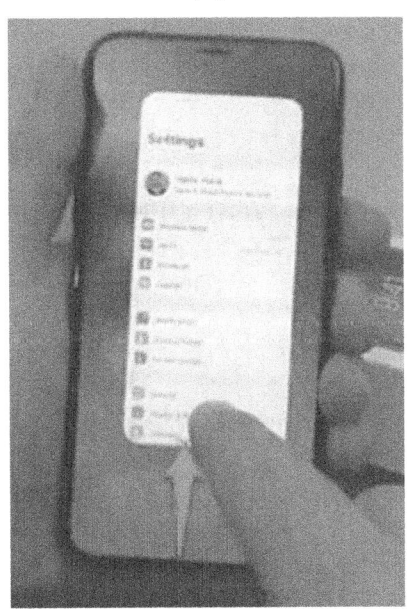

Hold and pull the bar up to display more opened apps

To go into the different apps, tap on it. To close any of the opened app, press and hold on it and it brings up the little red delete icon.

This doesn't delete the app but closes it. You can also swipe up to close a running app.

Emergency SOS

Press the side button and the volume up button at the same time. In addition to the slide to power OFF function, you also have access to the Emergency SOS. The emergency SOS is a very important feature. It has the potential to save you from a potentially dangerous situation. If you swipe the Emergency SOS, it will automatically call emergency services and also alert anyone in your health app listed as an emergency contact. Another way to set up access to the Emergency SOS service is by tapping the side button five times. However, you need to set it up.

Go to <u>Settings</u> › Emergency SOS › Enable the <u>Also works with 5 Clicks</u> by turning it ON. This way, you can access Emergency services much quicker by tapping the side button five times without having to swipe on your phone. This is valuable in a situation where you have your phone in your pocket and you encounter a dangerous situation that won't allow you bring it out.

Access Lock Screen

To access your lock screen, swipe down from the top left.

Access Control Center

To access the control center, swipe down from the top right. From here, you can quickly adjust settings and other handy iPhone features.

To go to the Home Screen

If you are in an application and you wish to go back to the Home Screen, Swipe up from the bottom-up and this gesture takes you straight to the home screen from any app. If you have multiple Home screen, swipe along the bottom edge will bring you back to your main Home Screen.

How to Access Notification Center

Swipe down from the top. Here, you will find any recent notification you may have missed including notifications set to deliver quietly. Swipe up from the bottom to go Home again.

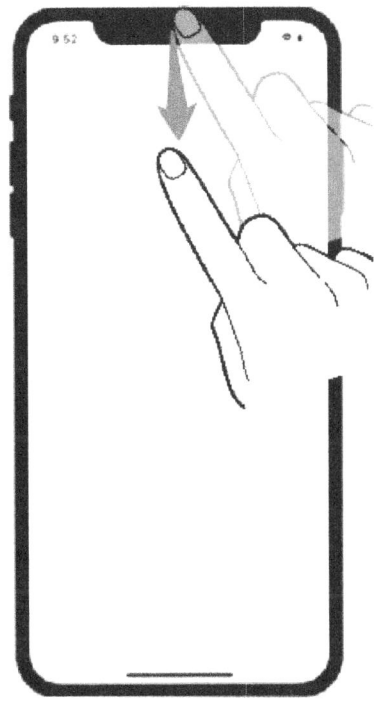

On the notification panel, if you press and hold any of the toggles holding groups of notification icons, it expands to give you more settings options.

To Search for Something Within the iPhone

Swipe down from the middle of the screen to bring up the spotlight search.

How to Add Card to Apple Pay

Mobile payment systemuses a technology called tokenization to keep card details secure. Once you add your card to the App, it generates a virtual account number and your real card number is never given to the merchants, it is encrpted. If your phone is stolen or misplaced, Apple Pay allows you to delete your account details remotely which will remove your virtual wallet along with it. Below are the steps to add a card to your Apple Pay Wallet

- Open wallet app

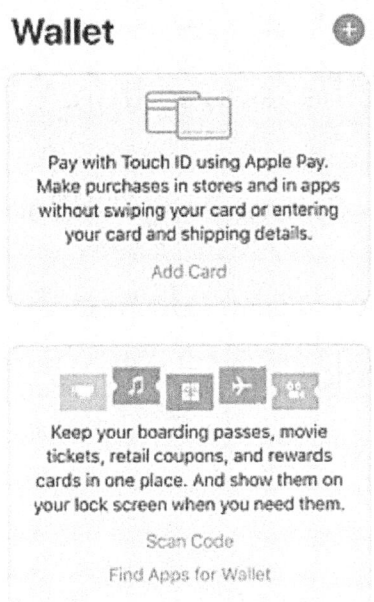

Wallet

Pay with Touch ID using Apple Pay. Make purchases in stores and in apps without swiping your card or entering your card and shipping details.

Add Card

Keep your boarding passes, movie tickets, retail coupons, and rewards cards in one place. And show them on your lock screen when you need them.

Scan Code

Find Apps for Wallet

- Tap ⊕ icon
- Scan your Debit or Credit Card
- Follow bank instructions 🏦 👍
- Done, your card is now added to the Wallet App and Credit/Debit card is ready for Apple Pay
- Double-press the side button. Use Face ID to authenticate then hold your iPhone close to the payment reader.

To put your iPhone to sleep

Single-press the side button.

To wake your iPhone

Tap screen or raise device to wake. Then use Face ID to unlock it.

3

Default Apps

In this chapter, we will take a look at the core apps on the iPhone 11, 11 Pro and 11 Pro Max.

Mail App

Tapping on the "Mail" app for the first time would present to you a "Welcome to Mail" page where you can log into your email account. Several email service providers are then presented to you to choose from, e.g. iCloud, Exchange, Google, Yahoo, AOL, Outlook, etc. For instance, if you have a Gmail, click on Google – type in your email, phone number and your password and tap NEXT. You will have your inbox content displayed after a successful login. This way you can keep in touch with your emails on your iPhone. You can send new emails, respond to emails, delete emails directly from your mail application. There is also a new text formatting tools to make emails look professional.

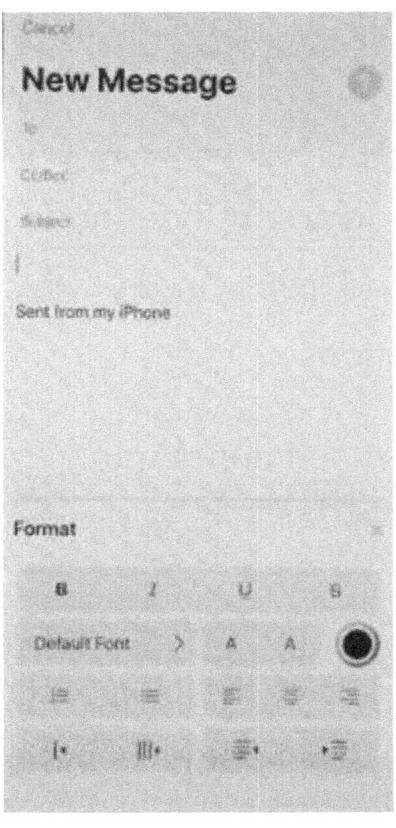

On the Keyboard for Message App, there is a new toolbar for inserting photos, drawing, scans and documents.

The messaging app on the iPhone 11 series also has an extended reply menu which gives you a lot of reply options.

Phone App

At the bottom left of the Home screen, we have the Phone app icon. Tapping on the phone app takes you to a keypad screen. Beneath the keypad are several options - favorite, Recent, Contact, keypads and voicemail.

• <u>Favorites:</u> This menu holds contacts you saved on your favorites list. Probably, people, you often call or friends and family members. You can add someone new from your contact to the favorite list by clicking the plus (+) icon at the top left of the "Favorites" window.

With this, you can dial whatever number you are looking to call.

• <u>Recent:</u> This holds the recently called phone numbers.

• <u>Contact</u>: This is the full list of your contact phone numbers saved on the phone. Tap on any of the names to give them a call.

• <u>Keypad</u>: The keypad enables you to dial phone numbers as well as save it to contact.

• <u>Voicemail</u>: This has voicemails left for you on your phone. Tap on the voicemail to also send a voicemail to your contacts.

Messages App

Tap on iMessage to compose a message. This displays as an iMessage if you are texting some-one that has an iPhone or a general text message to a non - iPhone user. There are more options when performing a haptic touch in the Messages App. For instance, haptic touch displays reply, reply all, forward, mark, notify me, mute, move message and archive message.

Safari

Safari is the default web browser for the iPhone. It enables users to carry out Google search as well as surf the internet by typing a web address into the URL. To switch between opened web pages on the Safari browser, click on the page switch icon ⬚ at the bottom right. To add a new tab, click on the plus (+) icon at the bottom of the page. Click on "Private" ⊞ New Private Tab at the bottom left to open a new private browsing window. To close a page, click on the "X" at the top left of each webpage. You can save a page to your favorite or bookmark a page by clicking on the bookmark icon . This opens a window which gives you several options on what to do with the webpage – you can either send it as a message or mail. You can also add it to your Bookmark, favorite or reading list.

Safari now has a new page-zoom feature at the upper left corner in iOS 13.1; with which you can zoom-in a web page up to 300 percent to get up close and personal with web contents. Underneath the zoom settings, you will find website view menu for invoking "Reader View" feature to adjust text size, background etc. You can also hide the toolbar and if possible, depending on the site you are on, request the desktop version of the website. You can also set the "Per-site" settings on Safari. This allows you to set a specific site feature. For instance, you can set specific sites to allow "Request Desktop Website" or Specific Site always "Use Reader mode Automatically." You can also change permissions on a per-site basis.

Another impressive feature of Safari on the iPhone 11 Series is the ability to save open tabs as a bookmark. When several webpages are open, you can bookmark all of them and place them in a folder by simply long pressing the bookmark icon and tap on "Add Bookmarks for 10 tabs" and tap "Save." In this instance, ten tabs were open and the entire ten tabs were bookmarked.

How to Adjust Photo Size Before Uploading on Safari

When uploading an image to any site via the Safari browser, you have the option to select between large, medium, small, and actual size of the photograph you intend to upload via Safari.

Calendar

This allows you to add calendar events into your phone. Just tap on a date or click on plus "+" to add a new event, then select the start time. The Calendar app can also be syn-chronized with Google Calendar in settings to ensure all events are available on the Calendar app.

Photos App

The Photo app shows you all of the photographs you have taken with your phone. Starting with the "Photos tab", it is a great way to get a high or low-level overview of your photos. In the photo's app, there are the "days," "months," "years," and the "All photos" section. This allows you to adjust your search or view based on what image you are looking for and when they were taken. The cool thing about "Days" is that it highlights the important photos and arranges them chronologically. The "All photos" allows you to view all the photos you have taken. You can zoom-in on the photos by tapping on the ellipses at the top right corner, then tap on the plus symbol or Zoom-out by tapping on the minus symbol. In the Photos app, videos and live photos automatically playback making the photos feel very much alive. To activate auto-play videos and live photos, go to "Settings" > "Messages" > tap "photos" > toggle ON "Auto Videos and Live Photos."

Tap on a photo to enter edit mode. In edit mode, you could pinch to zoom to get up close and personal to see those details, add filters and also adjust the intensity of filters to photos.

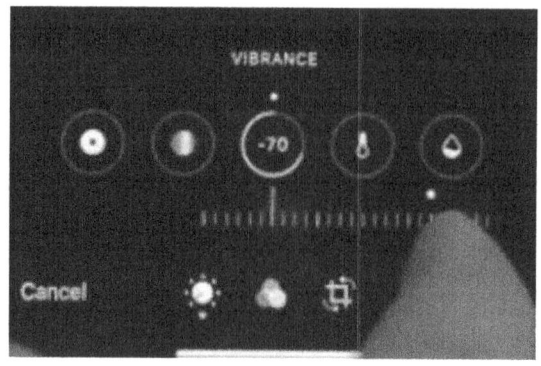

The "vibrance enhancement" allow you to boost colors without affecting skin tones.

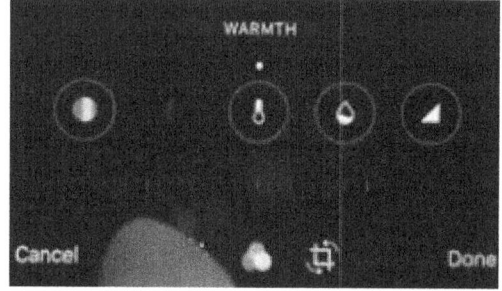

You can also fine-tune white balance by adjusting the Warmth & Tint balance.

Sharpen tool allow you to make edges in your photos crisper and better refined. The "Definition" tool allows you to adjust image clarity while the "Noise Reduction" tool allows you to reduce or eliminate graininess and spe-ckles within your photos.

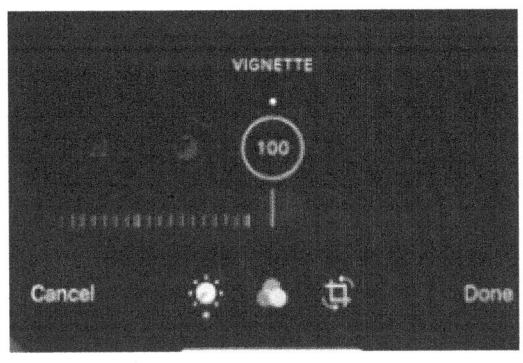

Vignette adds shadings to the edges of your photos to make your subject stand out. Note that you can review each of these effects individually. You can turn these effects ON or OFF by simply tapping on their icons.

Another addition to the photo editor is the "Portrait Lighting Control." The Portrait Lighting Control adjusts the position and intensity of each Portrait Lighting effect. So you can easily sharpen eyes or brighten and smooth facial features just like a photographer would in a photo studio.

Video Editor

You can do a lot of pro editing with the video editor on the iPhone 11, 11 Pro and 11 Pro Max. A key thing to note is that the video editing done on the iPhone 11 series video editor app are non-destructive. This means every change made to the video can be undone in reverse order. You have a full assortment of adjust tools with which to play around. You can trim, rotate, change vertical/horizontal tilt, flip, change aspect ratio (original, freeform, square 16:9, 10:8, 7:5, 4:3 etc), switch between portrait/landscape, turn Sound ON or Mute a video. You can also go into the editing interface, just like the photo editor and change the values of the effects. For instance, you can adjust the video's exposure, highlights, adjust shadows, saturation, vibrance, definition, vignette, sharpness, etc. You can also add filters and like the photo editing, you can adjust the intensity of the individual filters for the videos

Camera App

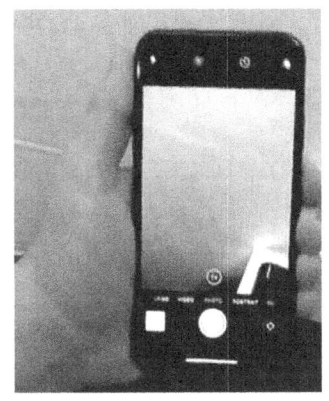

To take a regular photo with your camera, press the big white button at the bottom. Turn your phone horizontally to take landscape photos. You can also use the volume up button to take pictures as well. There are several features at the top of the camera. You can turn ON or OFF the flash using the flash icon ⚡ or keep it on "Auto". You can also turn ON/OFF HDR photos depending on the quality you are looking for, turn ON or OFF timer ⏱ if you want to set it up for a selfie or put it on a stand. On the top right is the filter icon to add different filters to your photograph. Also, you can zoom in and out by pinching your fingers on the camera screen. To change the focus point of your camera, tap on the position on the screen and the camera will focus on that point.

Take a selfie by turning the camera around to your face. Tap on the camera rotate button . There are other settings on the camera for quality photo shoot experience. E.g. time lapse (if you turn this ON, it would take a number of photos over a period of time which you can stitch together), portrait mode (it makes your photos come out better with different lighting effects i.e, studio lighting, contour lighting, stage lighting etc), Square (for Instagram), panoramic (takes several photos and stitch them together into one big panoramic photo). If you take a portrait mode photo, open it and tap on "Edit" to change the aperture from f16 to f1.4. This changes the amount of blur that is shown in the photo. To record a video within the photos app, press and hold the shutter button.

Swipe across the camera screen to go to video mode. This enables you to record videos. Tap on the red circular button to start recording. To stop recording, tap on the red circular button again. There are several options to choose from while recording. For instance – slow motion video (this is great for sports). At the top right of your video recording screen, it says HD and 60. What this means is that you are recording at 1080P which represents a High definition at 60 frames per second. The iPhone 11 Pro and Pro Max cameras are built to record up to 4k at 60 frames per second, but this is not set up by default. You have to go in and tweak the settings. To do this:

✓ Go to Settings
✓ Scroll down and tap on "Camera" option

✓ Tap "Record Video". This will allow you to pick between the different modes listed. (720p at 30fps, 1080p at 30fps, 1080p at 60fps, 4k at 60fps etc). Note: 4K at 60fps is only available at High-Efficiency Mode. The reason is that high efficiency takes less space on your iPhone. The higher the resolution and fps, the more storage space required. To activate the High-Efficiency Mode, tap on "Settings" > "Camera" > "Formats" - You will realize that the "Most Compatible" is enabled, this won't work for 4k at 60fps. Tap on "High Efficiency" to enable it.

Map App

The Map App is redesigned from the ground up in iPhone 11 Series. The Map app acts as a GPS. All you have to do on the map application is to search for an address, click Go and the app will give you step by step direction to get there. The Look around feature is another major addition to the Map app on iPhone 11 series. The Look around feature gives you a street view of selected areas on the map. Another fun feature of the Map app is "Collection." You can build a collection of favorite places and share those colle-ctions with friends.

Clock App

The clock app tells you the time for different locations/time zones. The Clock App on the iPhone 11 Series has a new splash screen and setup for Bedtime along with a slightly adjusted bedside tab at the bottom of the app. There is also an updated timer interface with a new circle that gives you a nice visual indication of how much time is left.

Alarm

You can set the alarm by going to the alarm app. Tap on Add Alarm to set up alarm time. You can have these alarms repeat. For instance, you can set the alarm to go off same time every weekday or every Tuesday. You can also change the sound of the alarm. Another option is to choose whether you want snooze to be an option or not. This is valuable now that Face ID is an option to unlock your phone. You can select the option to use your Face ID to snooze alarm. That way, you have to look straight at your phone to turn the alarm OFF; no more reaching to the side of your bed with sleepy eyes and pressing any button to snooze the alarm. Using Face ID to snooze an alarm will ensure you are awake. In addition to this, we have Bedtime.

Bedtime tracks when you go to bed, when you wake up and set up alarm that will correspond with that. This setting ensures you are getting the right amount of sleep each night.

Home App

The Home app allows you to connect and control any smart light, locks, or any smart technology you have in your home with the iPhone. Tap on the Home App icon in the Control Center to get started.

Note

This is an easy way to keep track of what is on your mind by jotting them down. You can also draw on your note and save them by clicking "Done."

Stocks

The stocks app allows you to track whatever stock you have invested in your stock portfolio.

Health App

Allows you to track your fitness over time. You can also add a medical ID to the health app. This way, if someone finds you in a medical situation, they can quickly get help with your medical ID. The health app works perfectly with the Apple Watch Series 4 and 5.

Apple Wallet

Apple Wallet app stores your credit card details so you can easily have access to it when you are tapping on one of those credit card terminals.

Calculator App

The calculator app allows you to do simple to some highly scientific calculations. If you turn your phone to the side while using the calculator app, you will get a scientific calculator which aids you to do more complex calculations.

Keynote

You can prepare slides for presentations in seminars or lectures with the aid of the Keynote app. It functions just like the Microsoft PowerPoint.

Downloading Apps from the App Store

To download additional apps into your phone, Go directly into the App store on your phone - you could either scroll through some suggested applications, check out the top free apps or purchase paid apps.

The Games Tab: This has all kinds of fun game apps you could download and install. Some are free while others are paid.

The App Tab: This has a list of useful iPhone 11 apps you could download.

Top Free: This is another way to get the top or most downloaded free apps. Click See All to see the entire free app list. Top free apps is a good indication of apps you should download in your iPhone.

Face ID & Passcode

Face ID is an enhanced security feature which identifies the face of the user before unlocking the phone. It provides secured access to app store, Apple pay, and authenticates user identity where ownership of the iPhone needs to be verified to prevent unauthorized access.

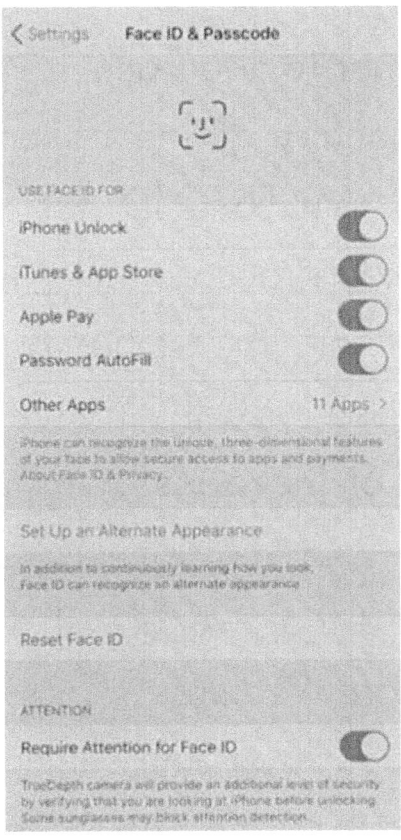

To set up your password and change your Face ID, open Settings > tap Face ID & Passcode > enter your passcode > You would be taken to a window to select apps that requires Face ID for access. E.g. iPhone lock, Apple Pay, iTunes & App Store, Safari AutoFill etc. ENABLE apps or functions from the list of apps that you would need Face ID to access.

If you don't want to use Face ID to access any app or function turn all the options OFF. If you are going to use Face ID for some options, adjust their sliders accordingly. Tap on "other Apps" to see all the other apps that are authorized to use Face ID. You can as well de-authorize any of the apps by turning Off their switch.

Another feature that works with Face ID is the "Attention Aware Features". Click on the "Face ID and passcode" from the settings menu, scroll down a bit, Enable the "Attention Aware features." when the Attention Aware features is enabled, the phone's backlight won't go dim or turn OFF as long as you are stiring at screen. It senses that you are looking at the phone and stays ON. Also, when you have this enabled, it prevent someone from using your face to unlock your phone while you are asleep. With this, Face ID recognizes your eyes are not open and won't unlock the phone.

If you need to "Reset" Face ID for any reason, click on the "Reset Face ID" button and it will automatically go through the process of setting up Face ID.

"Allow Access when locked" is a feature that allows you to set up apps and functions you can have access to when the phone is locked. There is a list of them which includes - Today's view, Recent notifications, Control Center, Siri, Replywith Message,Home Control,Return Missed Calls etc. You can Enable any of these functions to have access to them when the phone is locked. However, it is highly recommended to toggle OFF/disable all apps under the "ALLOW ACCESS WHEN LOCKED" feature. This is to

prevent unauthorized access to personal information on the phone.

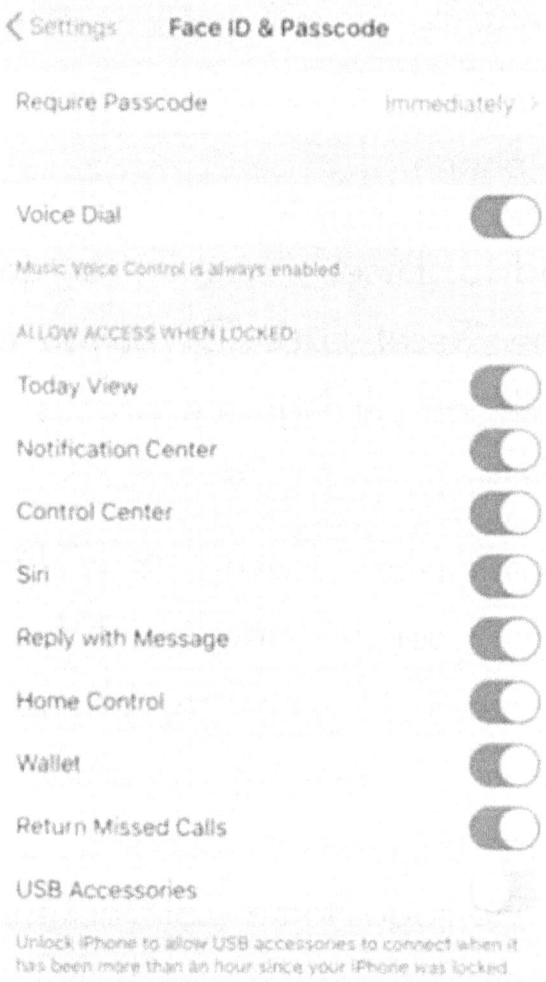

Finally, You can protect your data by erasing
them from the phone after ten failed attempts
to guess your passcodes. This will prevent unau-

thorized access to your data. Simply turn ON the "Erase Data" button.

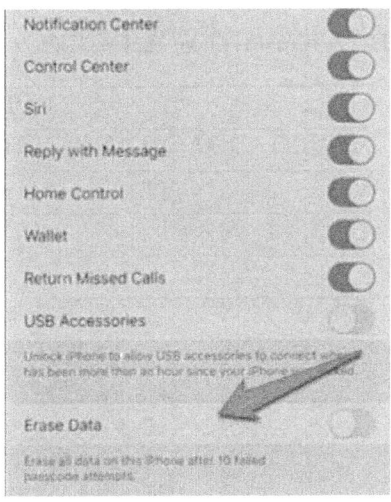

Lock Screen features

Swipe right from the "lock screen" to access recently used apps. Swiping to the left on the "lock screen" opens the camera app. Another way to access the camera is to tap on the camera app 📷 icon at the bottom right of the lock screen. At the bottom left is the flash light 🔦. Tap on it to turn ON/OFF flashlight on your phone. You can also turn ON/OFF the flashlight from the Control Center. The search bar at the top of the screen is used for searching through the phone for apps, messages, emails and virtually any information within the phone.

Changing Lock Screen and Home Screen Wallpapers

To change the wallpapers on your iPhone tap on Settings > click on Wallpaper > Choose a New wallpaper > there are several wallpapers to choose from (e.g, dynamic, still, live, etc.), tap on any of them you fancy > Set the selected wallpaper to either Lock Screen, Home Screen or Both i.e. <u>Set Lock Screen</u>, <u>Set Home Screen</u>, <u>Set Both</u> or <u>Cancel</u>.

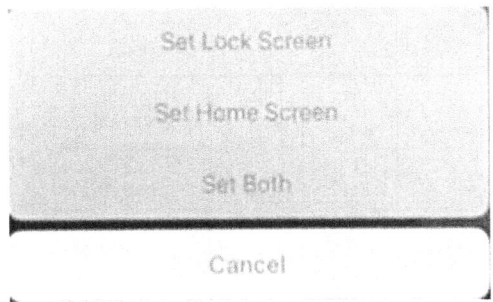

The Home screen is the screen you see behind all of your apps, while the lock screen is the screen that is displayed when the phone is locked.

4

Control Center

In this chapter, we will go through each of the control center icons and their functions as well as how to customize the control center.

To access the control center, swipe down from the top-right of your lock screen. The control center has a variety of different icons.

iPhone 11 Control Center

Airplane mode

Airplane mode allows you to turn OFF cellular, Wi-Fi and Bluetooth when you are in an airplane to prevent radio interference.

Cellular

This allows cellular service to be turned ON/ OFF.Turning OFF cellular fuction prevents phone from accessing your mobile service provider.

Bluetooth

Bluetooth connectivity allows you to connect your phone to an AirPod as well as connect to other Bluetooth devices such as wireless mouse, Game Controllers, etc. AirDrop also uses Bluetooth connectivity to share files between Apple devices.

Wi-Fi

Allows you to turn ON/OFF Wi-Fi connectivity. You can as well connect to a Wi-Fi network from the control panel.

Easy Access Control Panel

This is a little control panel that displays the current app using radio functionality. For instance, if you are listening to music or watching a YouTube video, this panel gives you control of the media playing without having to leave the control center.

Lock Rotation

When an iPhone is tilted horizontally, the screen display automatically changes its orientation to landscape. This returns to Portrait orientation when the phone is rotated to a vertical position. Activating the "rotation lock" locks the phone to portrait orientation irrespective of whether the phone is tilted horizontally or vertically.

Do not Disturb

The "Do not disturb" setting deactivates both visual and sound notifications from phones calls, text messages and other alerts. This is very useful when you are in a meeting, driving, or in a place where you don't want to be distracted. The "Do Not Disturb While Driving" is a great control feature. When this is enabled, it will automatically send a text message to anyone who calls, notifying them you are driving and would respond to their call whenever you get to your destination.

Brightness Settings

This allows you to increase or decrease the screen brightness. Haptic tap on the brightness icon to give you an option to turn ON/OFF "True Tone" as well as "Night Shift". True Tone takes the background lighting around you and adapts the iPhone screen to that automatically. Night Shift changes the tone of the screen depending on how well the room is lit in order to prevent glares from getting into your eyes. It also gets rids of some of the blue lights at the background to help your eyes adjust to the rays from the screen at night. This helps protect your eyes from light strains. You can also sche-dule the night shift option.

Volume Settings

The volume icon is used for increasing /decreasing the phone volume. Haptic tap on the icon to get more setting options.

Screen Mirroring

This allows you to mirror the screen of your phone on another device such as a laptop, projector, Television etc.

Low Power Mode

When this is enabled, it will save the phone's battery life by getting rid of some minor features in your phone that takes up a lot of batteries.

Other optional controls that can be added to the control center are the timer⏰,Flash light🔦, Calculator🔢, Camera📷 etc.

How to Customize the Control Center

You can customize the Control Center: Go to Settings > Control Center > Customize Controls. Here, you can add or remove control center features. To add more controls, click on the plus sign "+" beside the control. To remove an existing control feature, click on the minus "-" beside the control feature. Control features that can be added to the control center include Calculator, Camera, Screen Recording, Accessibility short-cuts, Alarm, Apple TV Remote, Do Not Disturb While Driving, Guided Access, Low Power Mode, Magnifier, Notes, etc.

5

Advanced Siri Commands

Siri has been around for a while, but it is easy to forget the basics of Siri commands. A lot can be done with Siri on the iPhone 11, 11 Pro and 11 Pro Max. Siri now sounds better in the iPhone 11 Series, thanks to the advanced neural text-to-speech technology that came with iOS 13.1. Apple also added a new Indian English accent for Siri for Indian Users of the iPhone 11 series. Other Accents include American, Australian, British, Irish and South African Accent.

Siri is activated by pressing and holding the power button and then say your command. Alternatively, it is activated by saying "Hey! Siri".

The list of Siri commands continues to grow and evolve with the continuous improvements and addition of new Siri commands. These new improvements in the voice recognition Artificial Intelligence Technology is geared towards making iPhone 11 users get better and more efficient ways to communicate with their iPhone using natural language. However, you can try new commands and don't have to say it exactly the way you see them in this manual. The list below is not exhaustive because new phrases are continuously being added to the Siri voice command.

Siri Basics

- List things you can ask Siri: {Hey Siri, what can I ask you?}
- When asking Siri for help: {"Hey Siri, help."}
- Getting into a conversation with Siri: {"Hey Siri, let's chat."}
- Changing Volume on the Phone: {"Hey Siri, set the volume to 5," " Hey Siri, louder" or "Hey Siri, turn up/down the volume."}
- Display photos: {"Hey Siri, show my photos" or, "Hey Siri, show me pictures of cats."}

- Ask Siri to display the weather forecast: {"Hey Siri, show me the weekend forecast."}
- Ask Siri to display food recipes: {"Hey Siri, show me a slow cooker recipe."}
- Ask Siri to Send a text Message {Hey Siri, send a text message to Michael} then dictate the text message to be sent to Michael.
- Instruct Siri to display timers: {"Hey Siri, show me my timers."}
- Use Siri to open an app:{"Hey Siri, open Uber."}
- Opening stored apps: {"Hey Siri, open [app name] " or "Hey Siri, launch [app name]"}
- Return iPhone to home screen: {"Hey Siri, return home."}
- Call someone on speaker mode: {"Hey Siri, call Maxwell on speaker."}
- Find out distance: {"Hey Siri, how far away is Chicago?"}
- Play Voicemail recording: {"Hey Siri, play my last voicemail"}

- Ask for Stock price: {"Hey Siri, what's the Apple stock at"}
- Read text messages: {"Hey Siri, read my last text message from Maxwel"}
- Send text messages: {Hey Siri, text mum saying we are on our way"}
- Know your exact location: {Hey Siri, where am i?"}
- Temperature conversion: {Hey Siri, what 75°C in Fahrenheit"}

Siri Language Translation

Hey Siri, translate "What time is it" to French

Hey Siri, say "this food is delicious" in Mandarin

Hey Siri, say "I Love you" in Spanish

Siri Media controls

- Siri command to play music: {"Hey Siri, play some music."}
- Place specific song or artist on a queue: {"Hey Siri, play music by [artist]."}

- Playing songs based on content: {"Hey Siri, play the latest Avett Brothers album" or "Hey Siri, play that song that goes 'Gotta gotta be down, because I want it all."}
- Playing music based on a theme: {"Hey Siri, play baby-making music" or "Hey Siri, play rock music for working."}
- Playing the song of the day: {"Hey Siri, play the song of the day."}
- Set a timer for sleep: {"Hey Siri set a sleep timer for 45 minutes" or "Hey Siri, stop playing in 45 minutes."}
- Get detail information about a song: {"Hey Siri, what's playing?"}
- Control Music: {"Hey Siri, play" or "Hey Siri, next."}
- Restart a song: {"Hey Siri, restart."}

Siri Time and date

- Setting an alarm: {"Hey Siri, set an alarm for 7 a.m." or "Hey Siri, wake me up at 7 in the morning."}
- Setting a music alarm: {"Hey Siri, wake me up to [artist, song, genre, playlist or album] at 8 a.m.," "Hey Siri, set an alarm to Band of Horses" or "Hey Siri, wake me up to Kiss FM on TuneIn."}
- Setting a repeating alarm: {"Hey Siri, set a repeating alarm for weekdays at 7 a.m."}
- Setting a timer: {"Hey Siri, timer" or "Hey Siri, set a timer for 15 minutes."}
- Create timer with a name: {"Hey Siri, set a pizza timer for 20 minutes."}
- Setting multiple timers: {"Hey Siri, set a second timer for 5 minutes."}
- Check timer status: {"Hey Siri, how much time is left on the pizza timer?" or "Hey Siri, what are my timers?"}

- Cancelling a timer: {"Hey Siri, cancel the pizza timer" or "Hey Siri, cancel the 15 - minute timer."}
- Ask for time: {"Hey Siri, what time is it?"}
- Ask for date: {"Hey Siri, what's the date?"}
- Cancel an alarm: {"Hey Siri, cancel my alarm for 3 p.m."}
- Snooze alarm: {"Hey Siri, snooze."}
- Check dates: {"Hey Siri, when is [holiday] this year?"}

Siri To-do and shopping lists

- Add task to to-do list: {"Hey Siri, add "go to the grocery store" to my to-do list" or "Hey Siri, I need to make an appointment with the doctor."}
- Create a new to-do item: {"Hey Siri, create a to-do."}
- Check events on calendar: {"Hey Siri, what's on my calendar for tomorrow?"}

- Scan QR Code: {Hey Siri!, Scan a QR code"}
- Add an event to calendar: {"Hey Siri, add [event] to my calendar for [day] at [time]" or "Hey Siri, add an event to my calendar."}
- Create a shopping list: {"Hey Siri, add eggs to my shopping list" or "Hey Siri, I need to buy laundry detergent."}
- Check shopping list: {"Hey Siri, what's on my shopping list?"}
- Create a reminder: {"Hey Siri, reminder" or "Hey Siri, remind me to check the oven in 5 minutes."} {"Hey Siri, remind me to pay my bills tomorrow"}
- Check existing reminders: {"Hey Siri, what are my reminders this weekend?" or "Hey Siri, what reminders do I have tomorrow?"}

Siri News and Weather

- Check News headlines: {"Hey Siri, what's in the news?"}

- Check the weather: {"Hey Siri, what's the weather like?" or "Hey Siri, will it rain today?" You can also ask "Hey Siri, will I need an umbrella today?"}
- Get weather forecast: {"Hey Siri, what's the weather going to be like this weekend?}
- Get update on traffic situation: {"Hey Siri, what's my commute look like?" or "Hey Siri, what's traffic like?"}

Siri Entertainment

- Search for movies to be screened at a nearby theaters: {"Hey Siri, what movies are playing?" or "Hey Siri, what action movies are playing tonight?"}
- Get information on moviesplaying: {"Hey Siri, tell me about the movie [title]."}
- Getmovie quotes:{"Hey Siri, give me a [movie] quote."}
Get IMDb rating: {"Hey Siri, what is the IMDb rating for [movie or TV show]?"}

- Get cast for a movie or show: {"Hey Siri, who plays in [movie or TV show]?"}
- Find out who an actor is: {"Hey Siri, who played [character] in [movie or TV show]?"}
- Find an actor's recent works: {"Hey Siri, what is [actor]'s latest movie?"}
- Find out who sang a song playing on your device or at random: {"Hey Siri, who sang the song [title]?"}
- Get the names of a musical band members: {"Hey Siri, who is in the band [name]?"}
- Get music album information: {"Hey Siri, what year did [band] release [song or album]?"}
- Find popular music by an artist: {"Hey Siri, what's popular from [artist]?"}
- Find sample music from an artist: {"Hey Siri, sample songs by [artist]."}
- Find an album or song: {"Hey Siri, find [song or album] by [artist]."}

- Scroll Left or Right: {"Hey Siri, scroll left or Hey Siri Scroll Right}
- Show available seasons of movies: {Hey Siri show me seasons"}

Siri Food and Businesses

- Get food recipes: {"Hey Siri, how do you make chocolate chip cookies?"} or {"Hey Siri, create a grocery list"}
- Locate a nearby restaurant: {"Hey Siri, find me a nearby pizza restaurant" or "Hey Siri, what's the nearest coffee shop?"}
- Get operating hours or a phone number for local businesses: {"Hey Siri, find the address for Bank of America" or "Hey Siri, find business hours for McDonald."}
- Get recipes for a meal {Hey Siri, what ingredients are in a Reuben sandwich"}

Siri Calculations/Conversions

- Convert units: {"Hey Siri, how many [units] are in [units]?"} {"Hey Siri, how many ounces are in a gallon?"}
- Convert units: {"Hey Siri, how many [units] are in 2 [units]?"}
- Basic mathematics: {"Hey Siri, what's 5 plus 7?" or "Hey Siri, what's 56 times 33?"}
- Advanced mathematics: {"Hey Siri, 70 factorials."}

Siri Definitions and Spellings

- Get the definition of a word: {"Hey Siri, what's the definition of [word]?"}
- Get the spelling of a word: {"Hey Siri, how do you spell [word]?"}

Siri Sports

- Check the results of a finished game: {"Hey Siri, what was the score of the [team] game?"}

- Ask if a team won a game: {"Hey Siri, did the [team] win?"}
- Ask when a team's next game is scheduled: {"Hey Siri, when do the [team] play next?"}
- Find out the results of your favorite teams: {"Hey Siri, give me my Sports Update."}
- Get Fantasy Football update with the Yahoo Fantasy Football skill: {"Hey Siri, ask Yahoo Fantasy Football for a score update" or "Hey Siri, ask Yahoo Fantasy Football if Colin Kaepernick is playing this week."}
- Get league standings of all teams: {"Hey Siri, what are the MLB standings?"}

Siri Search

- Get information on Wikipedia: {"Hey Siri, Wikipedia: [subject]."}
- Tell Siri to continue reading a Wikipedia entry: {"Hey Siri, tell me more."}
- Ask Siri a general question: {"Hey Siri, how tall is [person or object's name]?"}

- Ask a general question: {"Hey Siri, how many people live in America?"}
- Get a "Game of Thrones" quote: {"Hey Siri, give me a 'Game of Thrones' quote."}
- Search for Photos: Enable Siri and Search to be able to ask Siri to search for photos. Tap on Settings > "Siri & Search" > Enable "Search & Siri Suggestions" {"Hey Siri, show me the photos that were taken today."}
- Search for Apps: {Hey Siri, search the App Store for the best free games"}

Siri Holidays

- Find out when a holiday is: {"Hey Siri, when is [holiday]?"}
- Holiday limerick:{"Hey Siri, tell me a holiday limerick."}
- Learn about a holiday: {"Hey Siri, why do we celebrate [holiday]?"}

- Ask about Santa: {"Hey Siri, how old is Santa Claus?" "Hey Siri, is Santa Claus real?" or "Hey Siri, where does Santa Claus live?"}
- Ask about Santa's reindeer: {"Hey Siri, who's your favorite reindeer?" "Hey Siri, what can you tell me about Santa's reindeer?" or "Hey Siri, what do you know about Rudolph the red-nosed reindeer?"}
- Track Santa: {"Hey Siri, where is Santa?" or "Hey Siri, track Santa."}
- Sing a Christmas carol: {"Hey Siri, sing a Christmas carol."}
- Have Siri read "The Night Before Christmas": {"Hey Siri, read "The Night Before Christmas."}
- Spin the dreidel: {"Hey Siri, spin the dreidel ."}
- Ask for holiday jokes: {"Hey Siri, open my gift," "Hey Siri, how ugly is your/my holiday sweater?" or "Hey Siri, tell me a snowman joke."}

- Ask for holiday movies?:{"Hey Siri, what's your favorite holiday movie?" or "Hey Siri, what are the top holiday movies?"}

6

Sending iMessage/Animoji

In this chapter, we will look at how to send messages using iMessage and a feature called animoji. Go to the messages app > click on the contact of the person you wish to send a message to. If you want to send a new message, click on "Compose New Message" at the top right > type a regular message using the keypad or dictate a message using the dictate button 🎤 and click "send" > click on the emoji icon at the bottom left and select from the list of emojis. You can also send a text message with effect > type the message, force press the "Send" icon and it comes up with different text effect - e.g. Slam, loud, gentle, invisible ink, spotlight, etc.

Beyond regular typing, you can upload pictures or take a new one directly from the message app. By the side of the camera icon is a button Ⓐ which gives you access to additional features for the iMessage - i.e. new apps for iMessage, GIFs, Animoji, Digital touch (which allows you to draw or send drawing messages), music (which enables you to share music from the iMessage) and YouTube (will enable you to share YouTube videos).

Sending Animoji

Tap on Messages > Click on the Animoji icon > position your face in the yellow border to enable Animoji to track your face > Click on the record button and speak > Tap on the record button again to stop recording. The Animoji mimics your face and what you said. Click on the send button to send the Animoji via iMessage. There are different types of Animojis to pick from (e.g., cats, pandas, dogs, cows, mouse, octopus etc).

There are tons of new Memoji customizations for hairstyles, brows, eyes, piercings, facial hairs, ears, etc. You can also configure Airpods in the ear customization for your Memoji character.

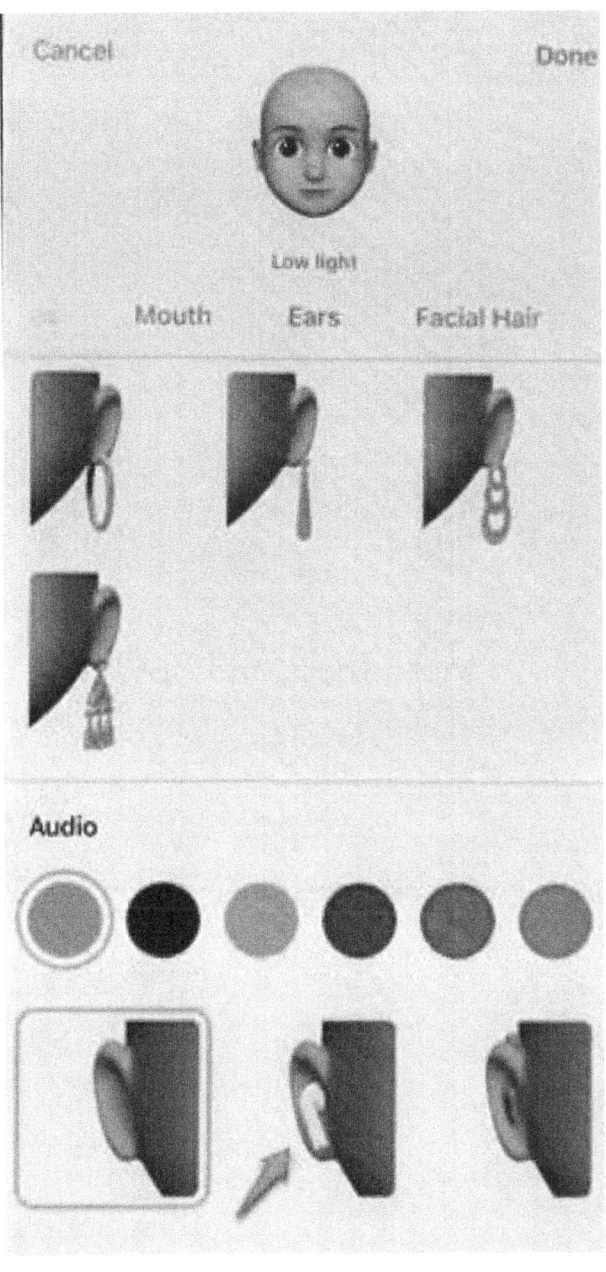

7

More Tricks and Tips

There are a lot of tips and tricks for the iPhone 11 Series. We will be looking at more of them in this chapter in a step by step approach.

How to set up "Hey Siri"

✓Go to Settings – tap on "Siri & Search"

✓Disable, then Enable the <u>Listen for "Hey Siri"</u> switch to set up "Hey Siri"

✓Tap on "Continue"

✓Say whatever is displayed on the screen

✓Click on DONE and swipe up to go to the Home page. Now, say Hey Siri, followed by voice command.

How to Activate AssistiveTouch

The AssistiveTouch is a shortcut icon which when enabled, appears to float on the screen. AssistiveTouch has menus for accessing Siri, Notification panel, Gestures, Control Center, taking a screenshot, Device options, Home button and lock screen.

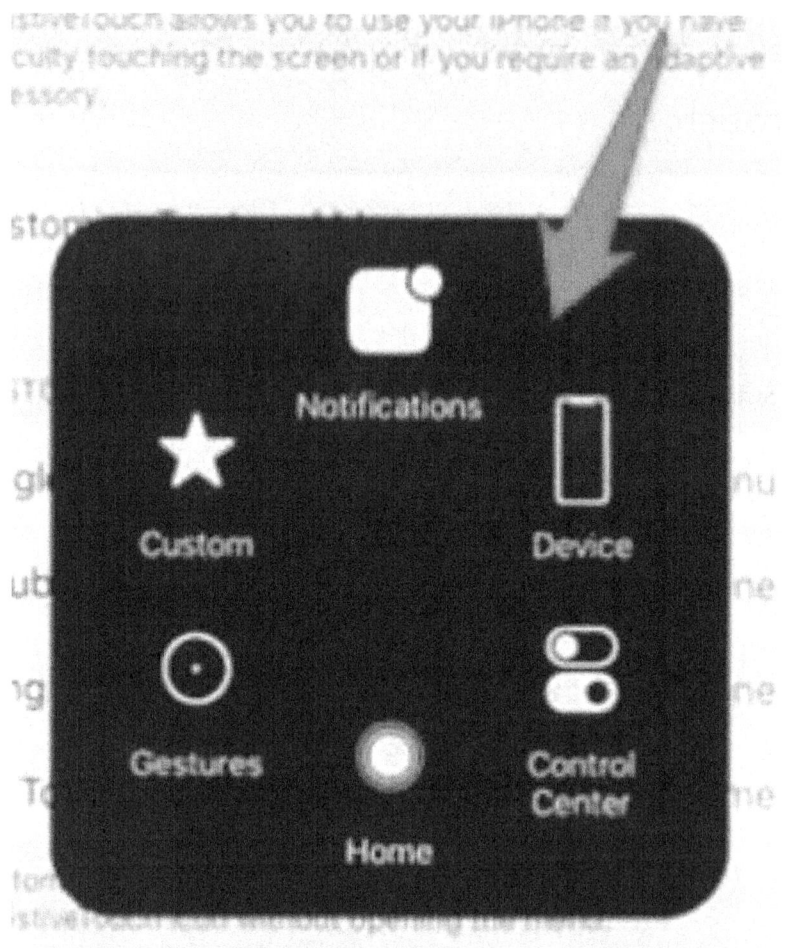

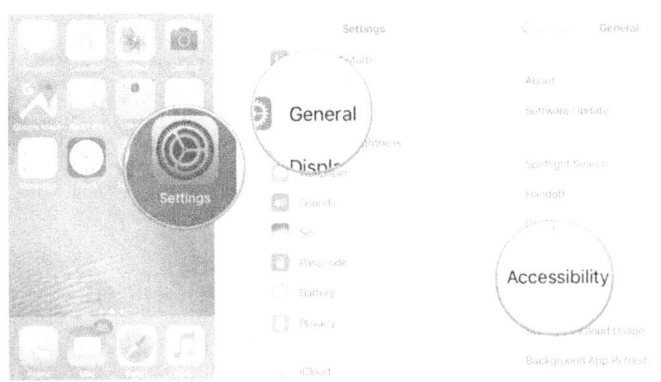

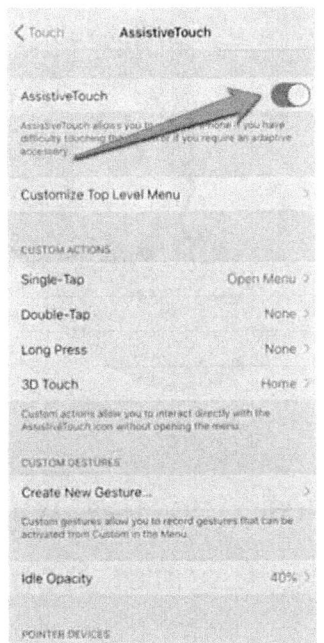

To activate AssistiveTouch, go to Settings > Tap Accessibility > tap "Touch" > tap Assistive-Touch and to enable it. This brings up the AssitiveTouch icon on the screen. Tap on the AssitiveTouch button to expand it. The Assistive-

Touch functionality is fully customizable, you can assign different functions to the AssitiveTouch buttons as well as add more buttons.

How to Connect Multiple Pairs of Airpods or Powerbeat Pro to the iPhone 11

Powerbeat Pro

While playing music on the Music App, Swipe down to open the Control Center > haptic tap on the Music app > tap the little Airdrop icon  on the top left of the music app > tap on the name of the two Airpods or powerbeat Pro and wait for them to connect to the iPhone. It connects and plays on both Airpods or the Airpod and the Powerbeat Pro simultaneously.

You can adjust volume independently between the two devices by adjusting their volume sliders. When both Airpods or Powerbeat Pros are connected, you see an icon 👥 on the volume button.

Siri also announces incoming messages on the Airpods when they are connected to the iPhone. You can also respond to messages simply by speaking back.

How to connect Playstation 4 and Xbox One S Bluetooth controllers to iPhone 11 For Gaming

Playstation 4 Wireless Console

You can use the Playstation 4 and Xbox One S Bluetooth controllers directly with you iPhone 11 series to play games that support wireless controllers. To link a wireless Playstation controller, to your iPhone, go to Settings > tap on "Bluetooth" to turn it ON > On the Playstation Console, Press and Hold the "Share" and "Playstation button" for 5 - 10 seconds > A pop-up (DUALSHOCK 4 Wireless Controller) comes up under "OTHER DEVICES" on the Bluetooth menu of your iPhone 11. > tap on the pop-up and the Controller connects to your iPhone. Now you can go ahead and play your games.

For Xbox One S Console

Xbox One S Console

On your iPhone, go to Settings > tap on "Bluetooth" to turn it ON > On the Xbox Console, Press the Xbox Button, then press and hold the back Sync Button on the Xbox Console for 3 - 5 seconds > A pop-up (Xbox Wireless Controller) comes up under "OTHER DEVICES" on the Bluetooth menu of your iPhone 11. > tap on the pop-up and the Controller connects to your iPhone. Now you can go ahead and play your games.

How to Optimize Battery Charging

The Optimized battery charging learns from your device usage routine and also helps reduce battery aging. To activate Optimized Battery charging go to Settings > tap "Battery" > tap "Battery Health" > toggle ON Optimized Battery Charging."

How to Add Emergency Contacts to Lock Screen

✓Launch the health app on your iPhone.
✓Tap on Medical ID at the bottom right

✓The tap "Create Medical ID."

✳ Medical ID

A Medical ID provides medical information about you that may be important in an emergency, like allergies and medical conditions.

The Medical ID can be accessed from the emergency dialer without unlocking your phone.

Create Medical ID

✓ Fill up your medical ID information

✓Toggle ON the "Show When Locked". If this is OFF, your Medical ID will not be visible on the lock screen. You must keep this toggle ON to enable the first responder helping you to contact your family in case of an accident or an emergency.

EMERGENCY ACCESS

Show When Locked

✓Insert the information that would be displayed on your medical record such as your name, date of birth, photograph, medical conditions, medical notes, allergies & reactions, medications, blood type, weight, height, organ donor, etc. After adding your medical information, the next section is the "Emergency Contact.

 add emergency contact

✓Click on "add emergency contact"

EMERGENCY CONTACTS

add emergency contact

Your emergency contacts will receive a message saying that you have called emergency services when you use Emergency SOS. Your current location will be included in these messages.

This will give you a list of contacts from your phone contacts. Select your emergency contacts from the list - for instance, your mum, dad, siblings or friends. It can be anyone.

✓Next, select your relationship with the contact you selected. This will help the first responder decide on who to call first based on the relationship status.

✓Click "Done" at the top right corner when all necessary information is filled out.

✓Go to locked screen and tap on "Emergency" and then "Medical ID."

✳ Medical ID

This displays the medical ID and the emergency contacts on the lockscreen. Tap on any of the emergency contacts to call them.

How to temporarily disable Emergency Contact from the lock Screen

✓Launch the Health app on your iPhone

✓Tap on Medical ID at he bottom right corner.

✓Scroll down all the way down to the bottom of the screen and tap Edit.

Edit

✓Toggle OFF "Show When Locked"

Show When Locked

✓Tap "Done"

✓Close the Health app and lock your iPhone. Tap on Emergency, but you won't find the Medical ID. These settings can be useful to hide your sensitive medical information from unauthorized access.

How to Delete Medical ID Permanently

✓Launch the health app on your iPhone

✓Tap "Medical ID"

✓Scroll down to the bottom and tap the "Edit" button.

✓Scroll down all the way to the bottom and tap on "Delete Medical ID.

Delete Medical ID

✓Confirm Delete Medical ID and your medical ID will be permanently deleted.

How To Add More Face IDs

Apple has added an alternate appearance to Face ID. It is a significant improvement to Apple's biometric security system. As of now, it allows a maximum of two users.

✓Go to "Settings" on your iPhone

✓Scroll down and Tap on "Face ID & Passcode"

✓Enter your passcode

✓Tap on "Set up and Alternate Appearance

✓Position your face in front on your device and tap "Get Started"

✓Then move your head slowly to complete the circle as the device scans your face.

✓Tap on "Continue" when you finish the first Face ID Scan.

✓Repeat the same process for the second time, and then tap on "Done" to complete Face ID set up.

To remove a Registered Face ID, Go to "Settings", tap on "Face ID and Passcode" and simply tap on "Reset Face ID."

How to Add More Friends to Group FaceTime

With Group FaceTime in iOS 13, you can quickly add a new friend to a conversation.

✓Tap the screen during your call and tap on the ellipses 🌑

✓Tap on the plus sign "+" to add another contact and choose who you want to call.

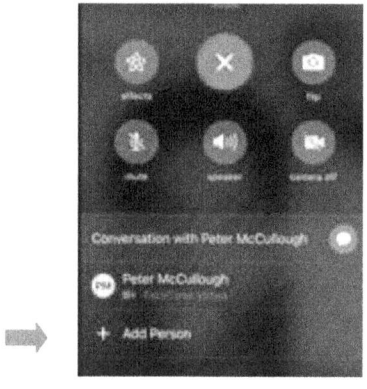

✓Tap "Add Person to FaceTime" and wait for them to join.

How to autosave and autofill login username and passwords on any website access on Safari

The autosave and autofill login feature works with the iCloud Keychain. To enable iCloud

Keychain, go to your Apple ID > tap on iCloud > go down to Keychain and turn ON iCloud Keychain. Now the iCloud Keychain is enabled. To enable the auto fill session tap on "Settings" ✓Next, tap on "Safari" > "Passwords & AutoFill" ✓Switch ON "Names and Passwords."

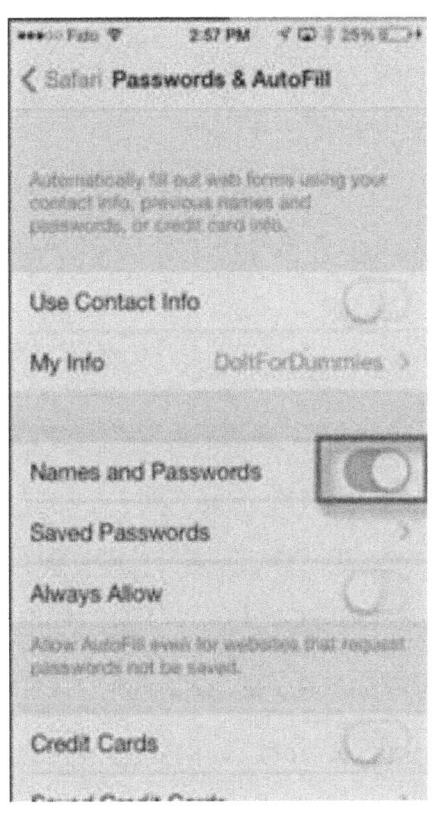

✓Also, enable "Credit Cards" if you want to autofill your credit card details on any website payment page.

✓To see how this works, open the Safari browser and go to any website login page. Log in as usual. You will be prompted to save the password.

> **Would you like to save this password?**
>
> You can view and remove saved passwords in the Passwords & AutoFill section of Safari settings.
>
> ### Save Password
>
> ### Never for This Website
>
> ### Not Now

✓Tap "Save Password". With this, anytime you log in that website's log in page, your username and password will be autofilled. All you need to do is tap "Sign in".

✓To view your list of saved passwords, go back to Safari Settings > tap on "Saved Passwords."

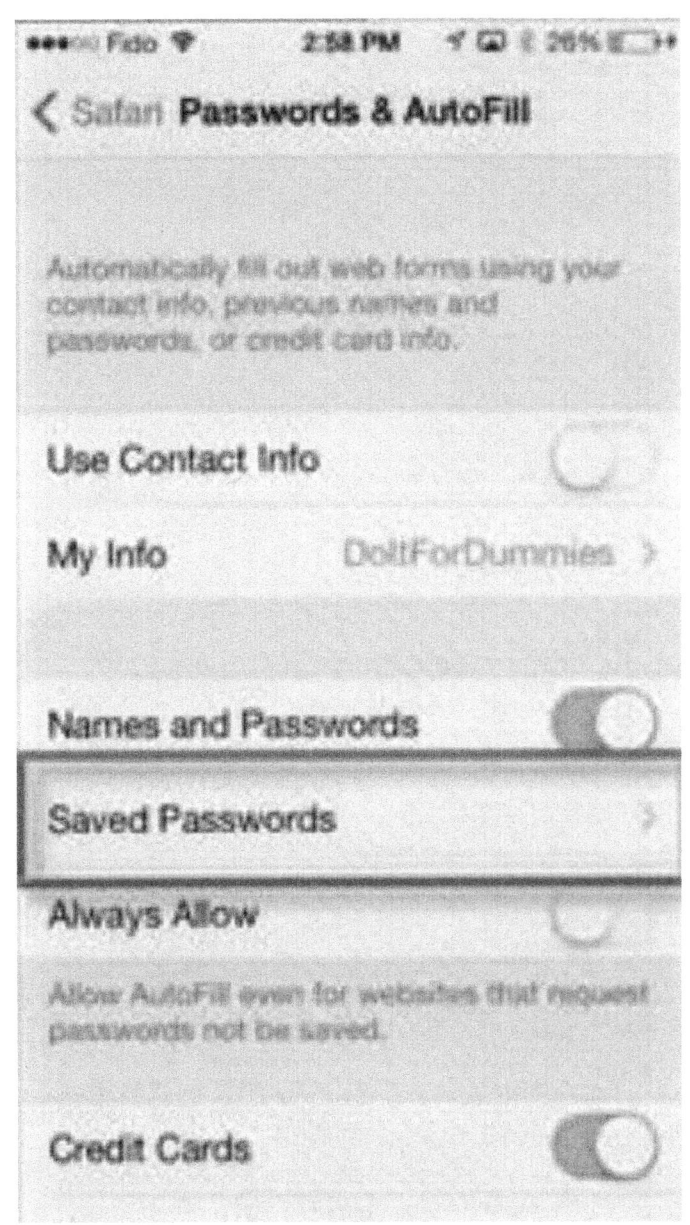

✓Tap on website to edit the password.

Here is a quick example of how the Safari

Credit card auto-fill works:

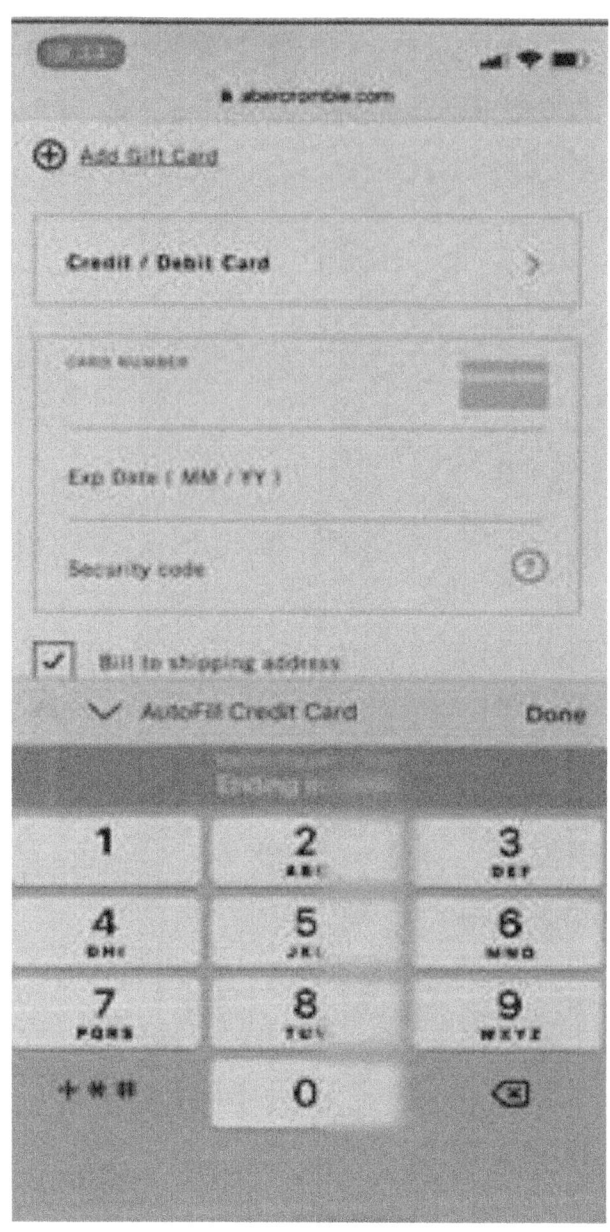

✓Click on a Card number and Autofill Card
number with Face ID comes up and the
Credit Card details is filled in.

How to Use Camera Effects

In iPhone 11, Apple released a new effects camera in the messages app with similar features that are found in Apps like Snapchat or Instagram. To access the new messages effects camera,

✓ Open the messages app and within the conversation select the camera icon ⬛ then select the star icon ⬛ in the bottom right corner to access the effects camera.

✓ From the effect camera, you will access various editing tools such as filters, text, shapes, stickers, animoji and memoji. Animoji and memoji will be available to you and can be placed over your face with the front-facing camera. The animoji and memoji filter is similar to the Snapchat filter and because it uses the true dot system, animoji and memoji stays lined up with your head while you move and talk mimicking your facial expression.

✓The filter offers fifteen various styles ranging anywhere from a monotone black and white filter to the comic book filter. Users can see these filters in real time to decide whether or not they would like to apply it before the photo is taken.

✓The upper and lower case "A" icon is reserved for text. Users can add text to their photos in various shapes or sizes.

✓"Shapes" is the scribbled line looking icon with which you have access to ten different animated shapes like arrows, scribbled lines, check marks and more. Shapes are static when used in photos but animated when used in videos.

✓Stickers can be placed on photos or videos and resized using pinch gestures. You can drag these stickers anywhere on the photo and reposition them using the same gestures you would use to put stickers within iMessages. For stickers and animate, you will see the animations when using them in video mode but there are no animations in photo mode. If you want to download more sticker packs, head back to your message conversation and select the App store icon to bring up the app store. From here you can browse various sticker packs which ranges from free to $1.99 on average.

✓Using multiple effect photo or video is also possible by simply selecting multiple effects and add them to your photo. For instance, you can use a memoji, comic book style filter and a text. To remove an effect for instance, a text, tap on the effect and tap on the "X" to delete.

✓Finally, you can change the exposure of a photo before taking it. First, tap on the object to focus the camera on it. Then swipe up or down to lighten or darken the exposure. If the exposure is too dark, you can brighten it and if it is too light, you can darken it. Another way you can do this is to press and hold the object on the screen to activate AE/AF lock mode. AE means Auto exposure and AF means Auto Focus. With this, you disable the automatic exposure and focus and then lock them in place.

How to Use Advanced Photography

This step is for advanced photographers who want full manual mode. That is you want to be able to control ISO, exposure, shutter speed manually as opposed to the camera app doing all that for you. However, to do this, you need to download Camera plus or Pro Camera App. I would recommend the Pro Camera App because it gives you full manual control over your camera as if you are using a DSLR camera.

At the bottom of the Pro Camera app, you have the exposure meter which enables you to change the exposure by sliding it either left or right. This makes the picture brighter or darker based on your needs.

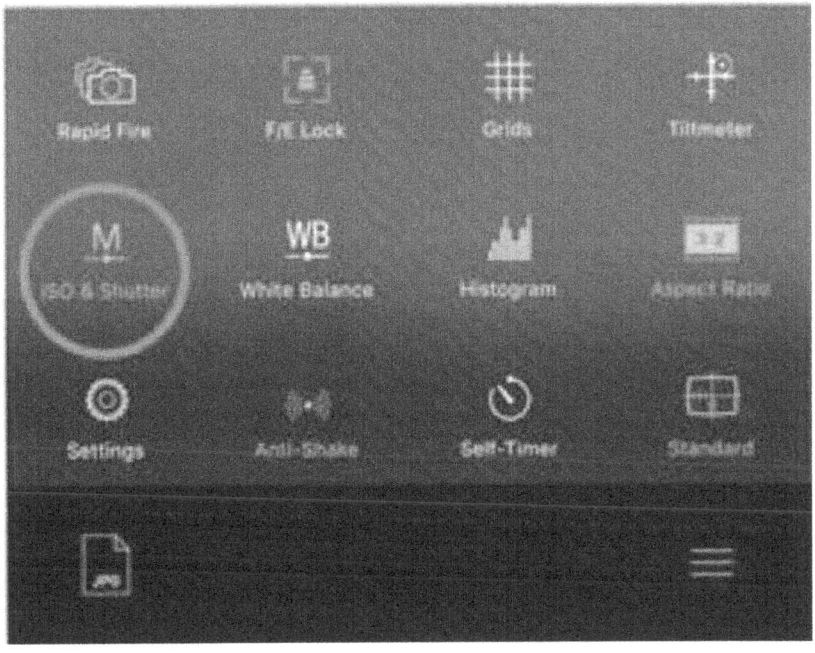

When you tap on the Pro Camera Settings Menu, you have several options:

ISO & Shutter Speed: With this, you can control the ISO and shutter speed of the camera manually. Displayed at the top of the ISO & Shutter speed window are Shutter speed, exposure value and the ISO value. Tap on each to make individual adjustments manually and then take a photo after that. Other manual settings you can do with the pro camera app are focus lock, select different grids, adjust tiltmeter (this shows you how leveled your camera is), etc.

How to Setup Notifications

Notifications are little reminders that show up on your screen when apps want your attention. When someone sends you a text message for example, a badge appears on your screen, when you swipe down from the top, the Notification center is revealed with all the notifications waiting for your attention.

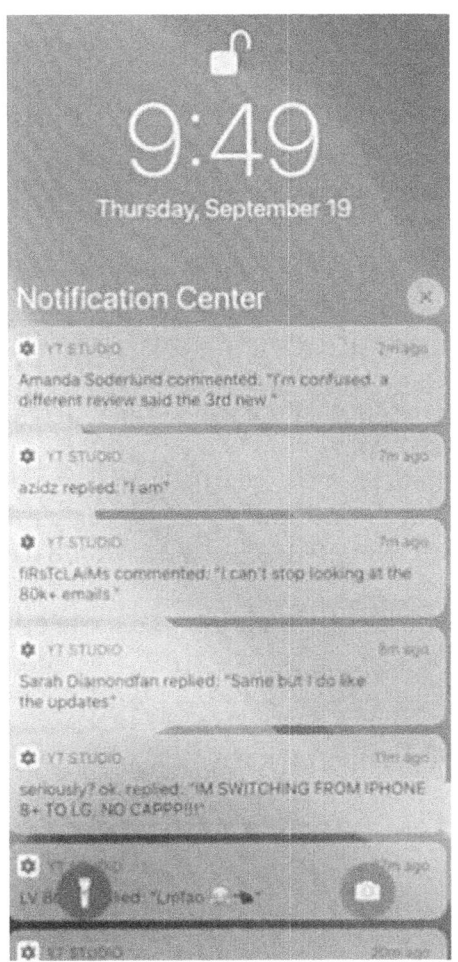

You can "manage," "view" or "clear" each of the notification by simply swiping it to the left to see the three options. When you tap "Manage," on a notification, you can do several other things from there. You can turn off notifications for that particular app for that particular app your are interacting with or you can access its settings option to make the app more customizable. Click on "View" to see details of that particular notification or "Clear" to delete it from the notification center.

Setting up a notification ensures you see only the ones you care about and lets you control how they appear on your phone. This way you don't get overwhelmed with notifi-cations you don't care about. To set up notifications,

- ✓ Open your SETTINGS app
- ✓ Tap on "Notifications"
- ✓ The next screen shows you all the apps that can send you notifications and you can control the settings for each one of them.
- ✓ For this example, let's choose how we want to receive text messages notification.
- ✓ Scroll downu and tap on "Messages."

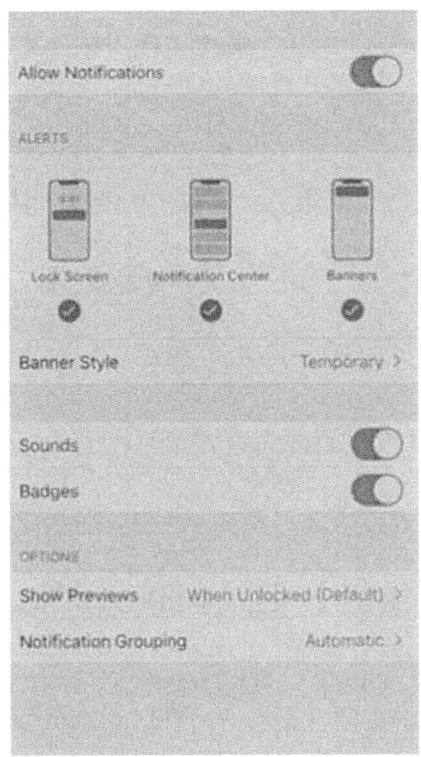

✓ "Allow notifications" let you decide if you want to receive notifications at all. If you don't want to receive any notifications at all from any app, tap the white circle, so the green goes away. That way, you have DISABLED notification for that particular app.

✓ The "Show in notification Center" option when toggled ON allows notifications from that app to be displayed in the notification center. You can access the notification center by swiping from top down on the home screen and a list of all your recent notifications will appear. This could be missed calls, an up-coming calendar event etc.

✓The next option you can customize is "Sound". Select it and a large list of sound is displayed. You can click through them and pre-hear each one until you find the one you prefer.

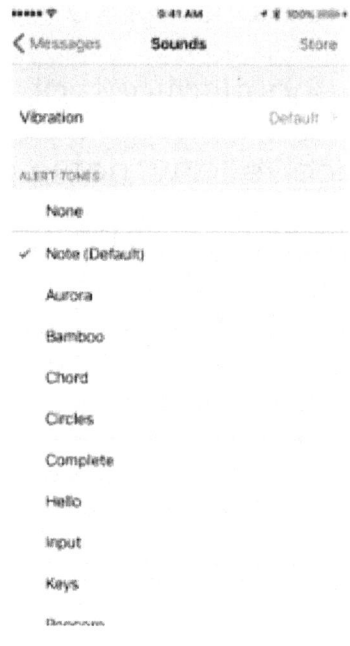

After choosing a sound, tap "messages" in the top left to return to the notification menu.

✓The next option helps you choose the style of notification. The first option is the badge. This notification puts a small red number  on your app icon on the home screen. This number tells you how many notifications in this app are waiting for you.

Badge App Icon

The second option is "Show on lock screen". When this is turned ON, notifications will show up on your lock screen.

Show on Lock Screen

Finally, you can choose your notification style, when your phone is unlocked. The first option is "None".

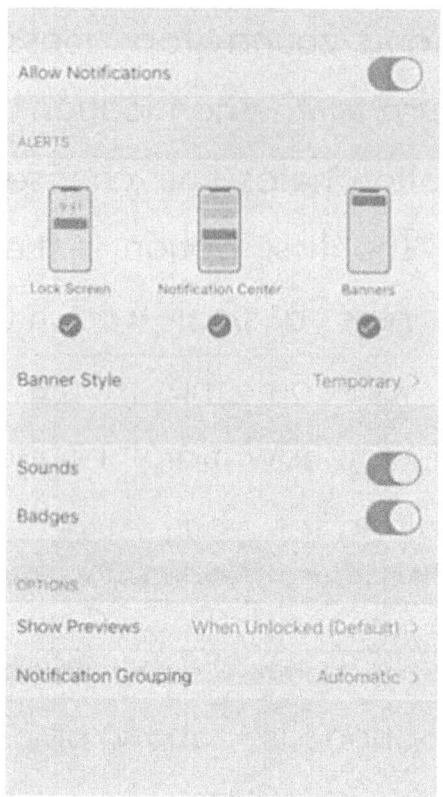

This will prevent any notification from showing on your screen while you are using your phone.

The second option is "Banner". A Banner will appear at the top of your screen and then disappear after a few seconds.

The third option is "Alerts". This puts a banner at the top of your screen that won't go away until you take action.

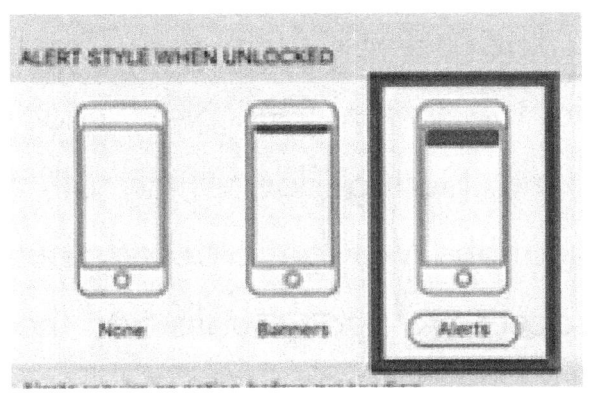

ALERT STYLE WHEN UNLOCKED

None   Banners   Alerts

At the bottom of the notification settings menu are two more options specific to the messages app. If you want to read some of the messages within the notification banner, tap "Show Preview" and then select "Always" or "When Unlocked". If you don't want to see the content of the message until you open it, select "OFF".

Finally, you can choose to repeat alerts, if you want to keep been reminded. You can control the notifications of different apps following the same steps enumerated above.

How to Use Downtime in Screen Time

Schedule time away from your phone to relax, enjoy family time or read that novel. Open

Settings > Tap Screen Time 🅧 > Tap Downtime and toggle the switch ON. Next, choose a start and end time. During down time, all your apps and notifications will be blocked. But you will still have access to phone calls and the apps on your allowed apps list > when you are done with the changes, tap "Screen Time" to go back.

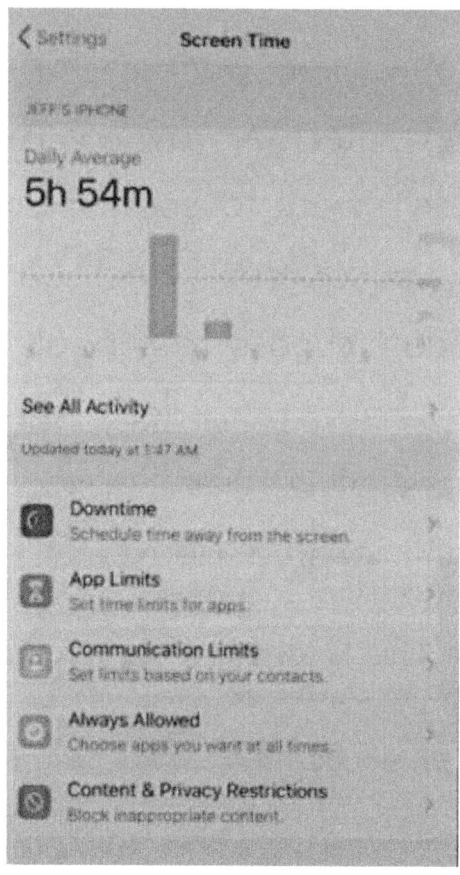

You can choose always allowed apps by Tapping the "Always Allowed ." Here, you will find a list of important apps you can still use during downtimes like phone, messages, FaceTime and Maps. If you want to remove an app from the list of "Always Allowed" apps, tap ● to remove an app.

To add another app to the "Always Allowed," scroll down and tap the green plus sign next to the app you want to allow. > Tap "Back" when you are done with the changes to your list. Now you are ready for downtime. When Downtime is active, the home screen dims all of your blocked apps and you will see an hourglass icon next to the app name. You will still receive notifications from the apps on your "Always Allowed" list but not from other apps.

Another important addition to "ScreenTime" on the iPhone 11 series is "Communication Limits." Communication Limits set limits based on your contacts. For instance, "During Allowed ScreenTime" you can allow everyone to be able to reach you or set people on your contact list only to have access to you. You can also allow only specific people to be able to communicate with you during down time. Tap on Settings > "ScreenTime" > tap on "Communications Limits" > "During Downtime > "Specific Contacts" > Under the "ALLOWED CONTACTS," tap "Add Contacts" to add contacts individually.

"Combine Apps Limits," allow you to combine multiple apps and add a limit to the group of Apps. Tap on Settings > "Screen Time" > "Apps Limits" > tap "Add Limits" > tap on the apps to combine them and set limits to the selected Apps. > tap "Add."

How to bypass Downtime Limits

If you try to open an app when it is unavailable, you will see a time limit warning. You can still use the app. Tap "Ignore Limit". Tap "Remind Me in 15 Minutes" to snooze. This allow you use the app for a little while > Tap "Ignore Limit For Today" to completely unlock it > You can tap "Cancel" to accept limit and move on.

How to have backups to your Photos and Videos on iCloud

There are a couple of things you can tweak on the photo library and one of them is to enable iCloud photo library. To ensure all your photos and videos are backed up to the iCloud,

✓ Go to Settings

✓ Tap on Photos

✓ Enable iCloud Photo Library.

How to Use the Measure App

✓ Open the measure app to get started.

✓ Some instructions will appear on your screen, telling you to move your iPhone around for the app to do a quick scan of objects around you.

✓ Move your iPhone around until a circle appears on the screen

✓ Move your device to get to the starting point of what you intend to measure in the middle of your screen.

✓ Then tap the plus "+" sign at the bottom to add a point. If you make a mistake, tap the undo button at the top left corner to try again.

✓ Move your iPhone so that the end point of the object you are measuring appears on your screen.

✓ Tap the plus "+" sign again to mark the end of your measurement. You can create multiple line measurements at the same time if you are measuring the dimension of an object.

✓ You can also tap on the measurement to see different conversions to other units of measurement.

✓ Tap "Clear" at the top right corner of your screen to clear all measurements or start over.

✓The app can automatically detect rectangles. If you move the camera over an object with rectangular shape; an orange outline appear around it.

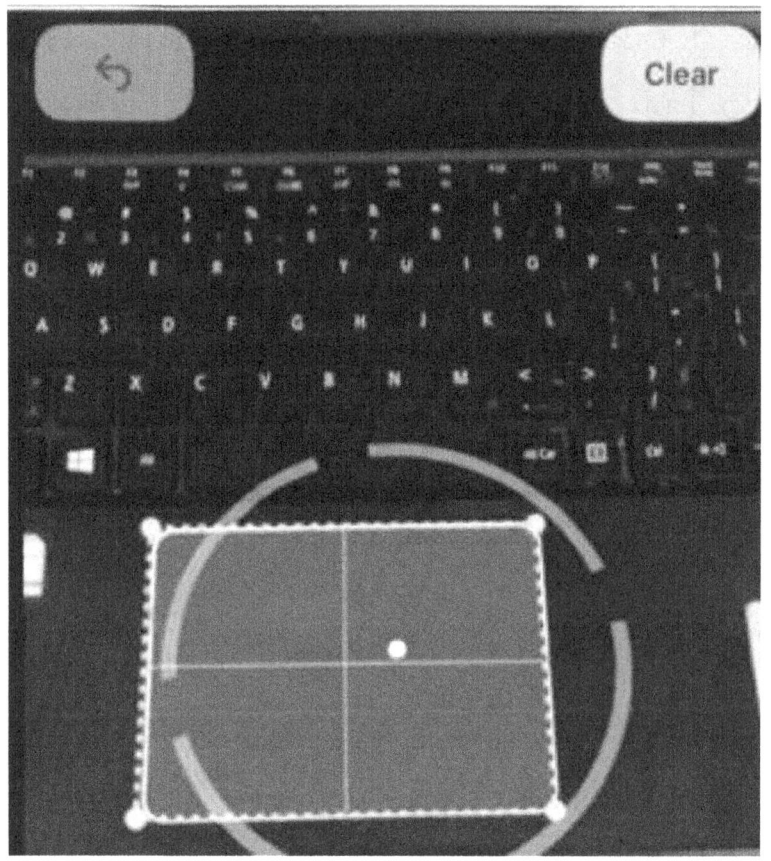

Tap the middle of the outline to quickly get the length and width of the rectangle at the same time.

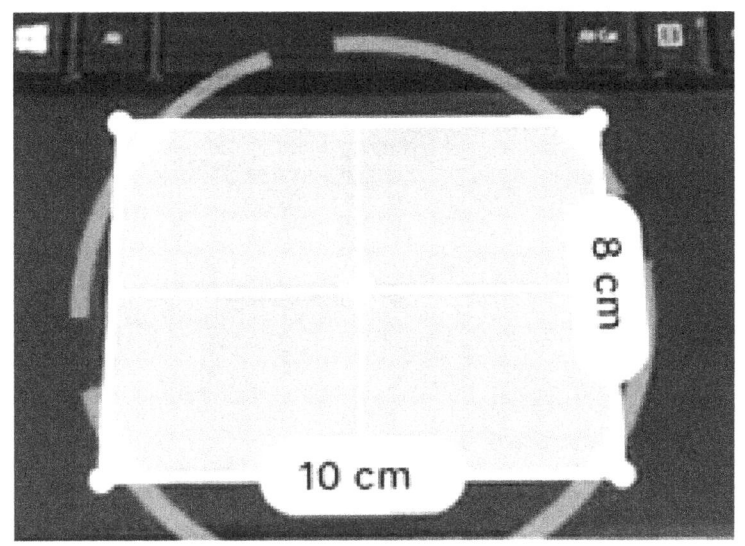

✓Besides measuring length, you can use this app as a balancing tool. Tap "Level" at the bottom of the screen to switch to "level mode." You can use this feature with your device vertically or horizontally.

✓Set your iPhone on a surface, you intend to get leveled. For instance a picture frame or a shelf.

✓When you tilt the iPhone, it tells you how many degrees you are from being leveled. When it is level, your screen will read 0° and the background will turn from black to green.

How to Remove Used Pass

The Wallet app is one of the ways to integrate Applepay into your iPhone. Applypay is the best way you can opt to pay for items using your iPhone. You can also use it to store different passes (e.g. links to hotels, boarding tickets for flight etc).

✓Open the wallet app

✓Tap on your card and your passes is displayed at the bottom.

✓Tap on the pass

✓Tap on the "i" 🄘 option at the bottom right.

✓Scroll down and tap on "Remove Pass". This will automatically remove it from the app.

How to Activate Low Data Mode

Low data mode helps apps on your phone use lesser Network Data. To activate Low Data Mode go to Settings > tap on "Cellular > tap "Cellular data options" > Enable "Low Data Mode."

How to take Screenshots on your iPhone 11

To take a screenshot on your phone, Press the Volume up and the Power button simultaneously and let go immediately. The screenshot taken is displayed at the lower-left corner of the screen. Tap on the image to display several annotation tools such as a ruler, pen and eraser that can be used to customize the image.

Tap on the "Done" button when you are done customizing the image. You also have options to save the file to photo, save to file or delete screenshot. The edited image is sent auto-matically to the photo gallery

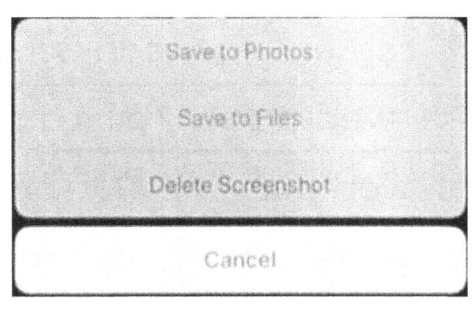

Alternatively, you can take a screenshot using the following steps; Tap on "Settings" > "accessibility" > "AssistiveTouch" > Toggle ON the AssistiveTouch. A grey floaty icon pops up on the screen > Tap on "Single-Tap," then scroll down and tap on "Screenshot." Go back to the Home menu or the page you wish to screenshot and click on the Grey floaty icon once.

How to Screenshot an entire Web page on Safari

Apple has support for full web page screenshot on the iPhone 11. To do this, open a web page on Safari > press the Volume Up and Power button at the same time and quickly release it > tap the screenshot image at the lower-left corner of the screen > tap on "Full Screen" at the top right corner. You can scroll down to view the entire web page. You can also export the screenshot web page to PDF by tapping the "Share" button.

How to Record Your Screen on iPhone 11

Besides taking screenshots on your phone, you could also record the phone screen while performing specofic actions or in-game mode. To record your phone screen, pull down the Control center > haptic tap the "Record Button" to expand the options.

From the options listed, tap "Start recording." A count down is set off, and then the screen recording is activated. At this point, whatever you do on the screen is recorded and saved in the photo's application. You can choose to send the clip from screen record to the Messager app. To do this, tap on "Messenger," then tap "Start Broadcast."

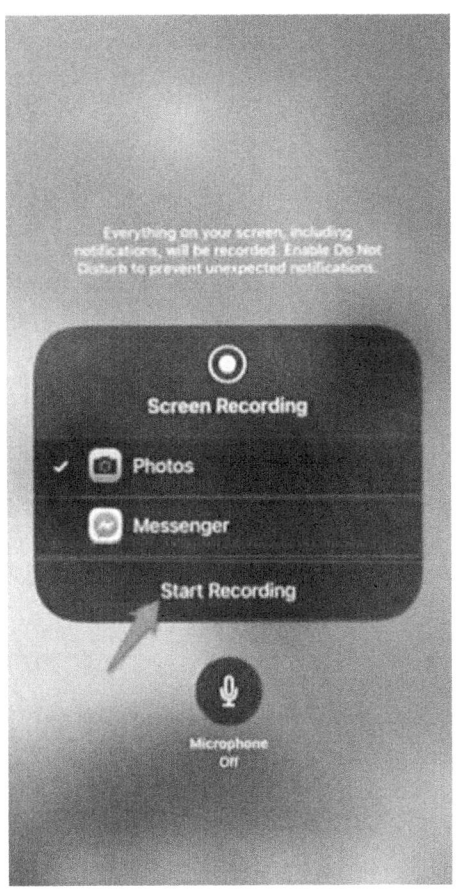

You can stop screen recording by tapping on the red button with the timer at the top left of the screen, then tap on the "Stop" button that pops up on the screen.

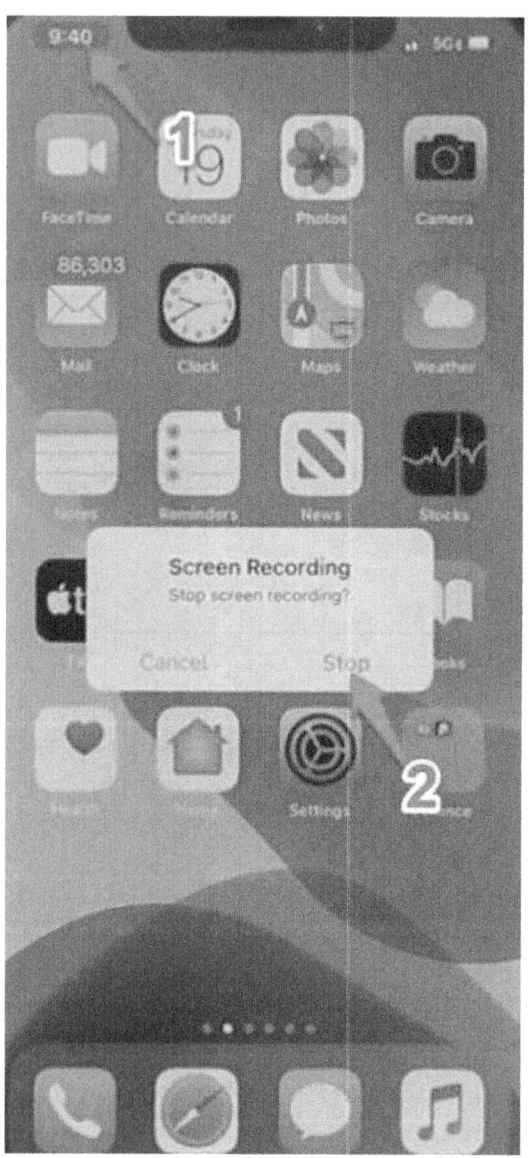

How to use Keyboard as a trackpad

You can correct a portion of a text message or a wrongly typed web address by pressing and holding on your keypad then, drag the cursor to the precise position where the error was made to modify it.

How to jump to the top of a page from the bottom

You can move right to the top of a page if you have scrolled down to the bottom of a lengthy. Instead of manually swiping down to the top of the page, tap on either side of the screen next to the notch.

This takes you right up to the top of the page in a second. This tip works for every location you find yourself in the iPhone including web pages. How to activate Accessibility Shortcuts From the Side button

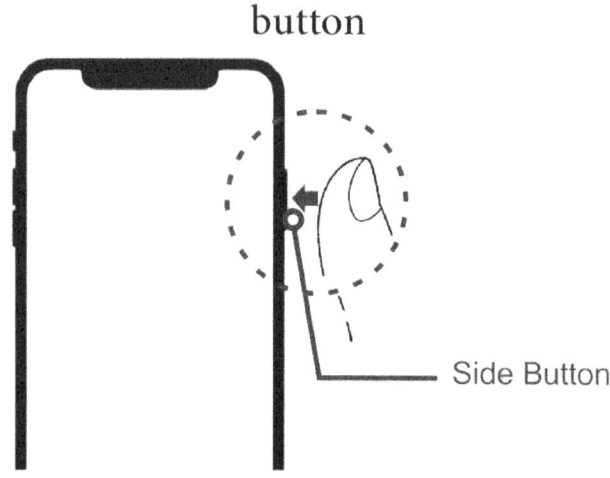

Side Button

You can set up accessibility shortcuts by triple-clicking the side button for either of the following – AssistiveTouch, Classic Invert Colors, Color Filters, Reduce White Point, Smart Invert Colors, Switch Control, VoiceOver or Zoom.

✓Go to Settings

✓Tap on accessibility

✓Scroll down to "Accessibility Shortcut."

✓For the "Triple-Click the Side button For", select an option you need triple clicking side button should activate. You could check all the options, but triple clicking the side button would request you pick from the eight accessibility shortcut options.

How to create Secure notes

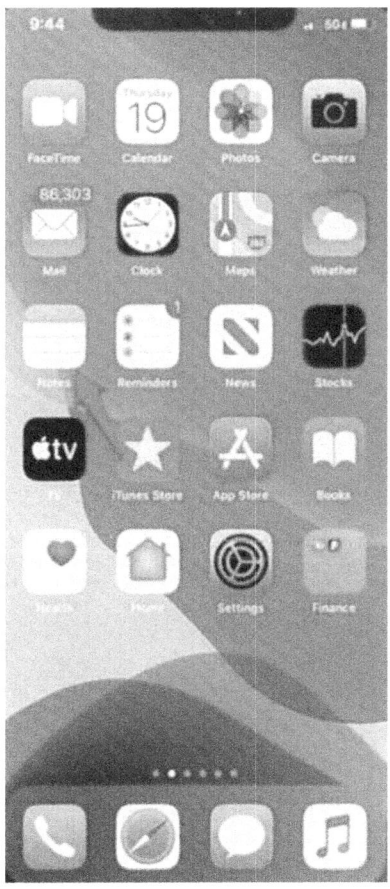

You can create secured notes that requires a password for access. To create a secure Note; Launch the "Note Application" > Create a New note > Tap on the share button 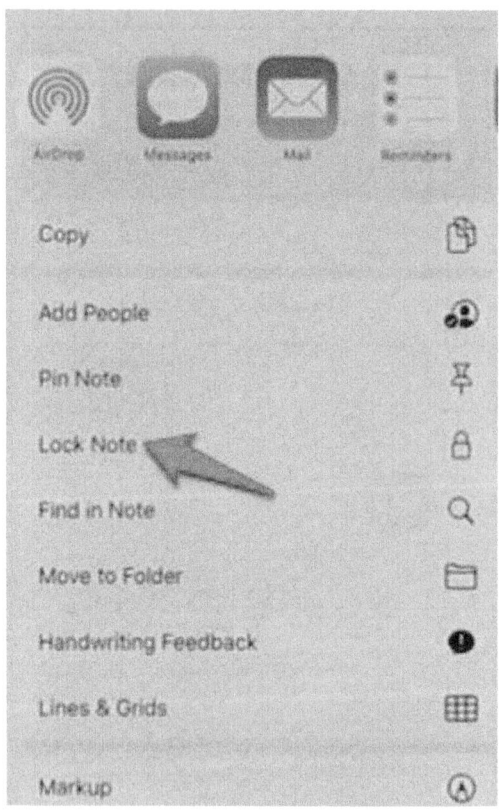 at the top right-corner of the Note App and at the bottom, you will find several options including "Lock Note."

Tap on "Lock Note". You will be requested to scan your face if you have the Face ID enabled or you can put in your passcode and the lock would be added. You would need to unlock the note using either Face ID or passcode to view its content. If you are doing this for the first time, you will be requested to enter a unique pass-code for your Notes. If you want to change your Note passcode, got to Settings > tap on "Notes" > tap on "Password"

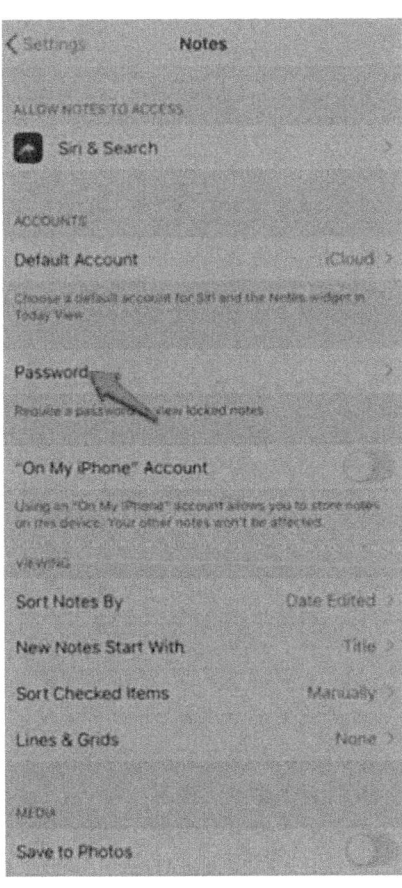

Tap on "Change Password" to change the passwords for your secured Notes. You can also Pin important Notes to the top of the list on the Notes App by opening the Note App > tap on the share icon > scroll down and tap on "Pin Note." Multiple Notes can be pinned to the top following this step.

How to Check Available Storage on the iPhone 11

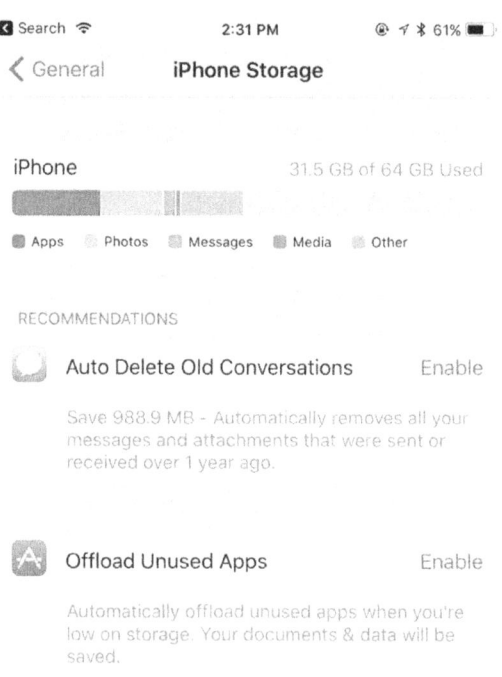

To find out how much storage space is available on the iPhone 11 series and a breakdown of how the iPhone's storage is being used, go to settings > scroll down and tap "General" > finally, tap on iPhone Storage. When you scroll down a bit, you see what applications are taking most of the actual space.

You can also delete applications from this menu. To do this, Tap on the app you wish to delete > tap "Delete App." This action deletes the selected app and all related data from the iPhone. Be very careful, because the delete action cannot be undone.

How to increase iCloud Storage

The iPhone 11 series comes with a default 5GB storage iCloud Storage. You can expand this by up to 50GB for just $1 a month.
✓Tap on Settings
✓Tap on your Apple ID
✓Tap on iCloud

✓Tap on Manage storage > tap "Change Storage plan". This takes you to a screen which allows you to purchase more storage. You can get 200GB for $3 a month and 2TB for $9.99 a month. Tap on the option that suits your storage needs and hit the "Buy" button.

How to set up two-factor authentication

This is a security measure for iCloud services that request for two things instead of a single password to log into an online service. Typically, the two-factors are usually a passcode and a code that the server sends to you via a cell phone. Requesting for two-factors instead of one enhances the security of your phone and prevents unauthorized access to datd on the phone. The following steps enable you to set it up via iCloud.

✓Sign into your iCloud account

✓Click on your username at the upper right-hand corner and from the drop-down, click on "Account Settings."

✓Click on your Apple ID and this would launch a new tab on the Apple ID page. Click on "Manage your Apple ID"

✓You would be required to sign in again.

✓Click on "Passwords and Security." At this point, you will have to answer some security questions and click on "Continue". You would be taken to a 3 step notification screen on the risks of two-factor authentication.

✓Next, click on "Add a phone number." This is the phone number through which Apple will sends aauthentication codes. Ideally, it should be your iPhone or any phone that you would always have with you.

✓Click "Next." This introduces a window that asks for your four-digit verification code sent to the phone number you added. Click on "Verify"

✓Add an iPad or phone or both to the list of verification devices. What this does amongst other things is it allows Apple to send verification code by push notification instead of just SMS. Once again you will get a verification code sent to your phone, enter it in the space provided and click on "Verify".

✓Get the "Recovery Key" that is displayed on the screen. The Recovery Key is another code you can use to unlock your iCloud account if you don't have your phone with you. You will be able to log in with this verification key and your password. It is always adviced that you print out the recovery key and keep it in a safe place.

✓Click "Done" to activate two-step verification and whenever you log into iCloud.com to manage your account or make purchase from a new device, get Apple ID - related support or use one of Apples web apps on iCloud.com, Apple will check to ensure you are who you say you are by sending a verification code to the phone your registered plus your usual password to get in.

How to Enable Dark Mode

Dark mode gives Apple's pre-installed apps on the iPhone 11 a dark background and a little aesthetics as well. Activating dark mode on the phone also preserves battery life. To activate dark mode,

✓Go to Settings

✓Scroll down and tap on "Display & Brightness."

✓On the top you have the quick toggle that allows you to switch between light and dark. Select "Dark" and everything turns into dark mode.

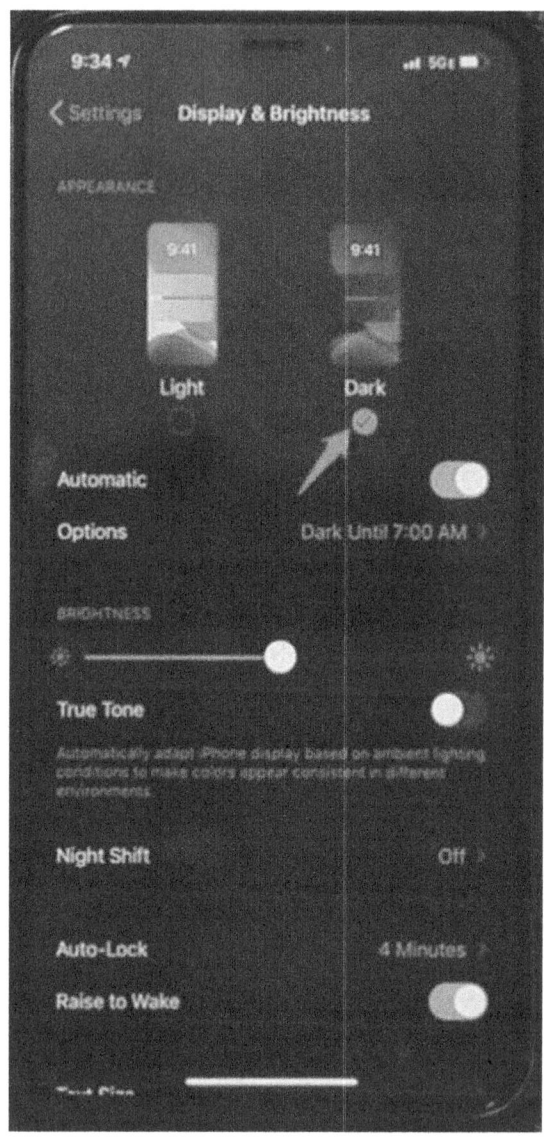

✓Alternatively, you can activate dark mode from the Control center by pressing and holding the screen brightness icon, then tap on dark mode at the lower-left corner.

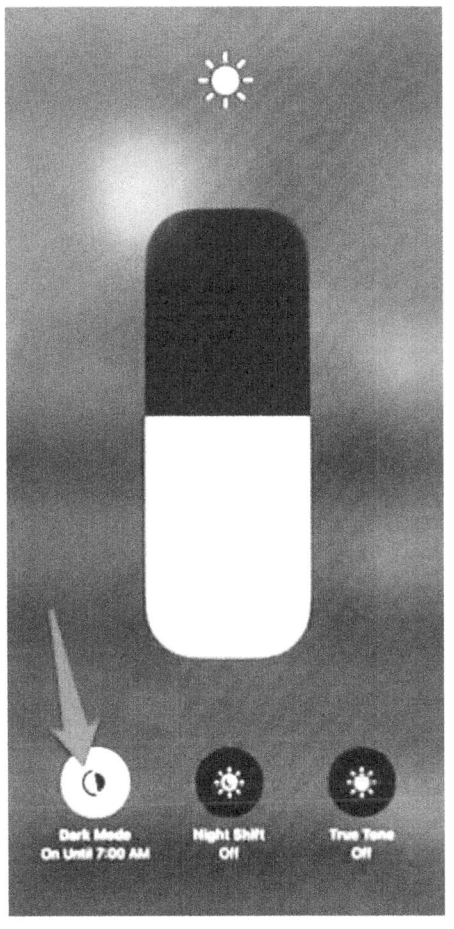

A quicker way to activate Dark Mode is to tap on the dark mode icon ◐ directly from the Control center. If the dark mode icon is not displayed in the control center, to add it go to settings › Control Center › tap on "Customize controls."

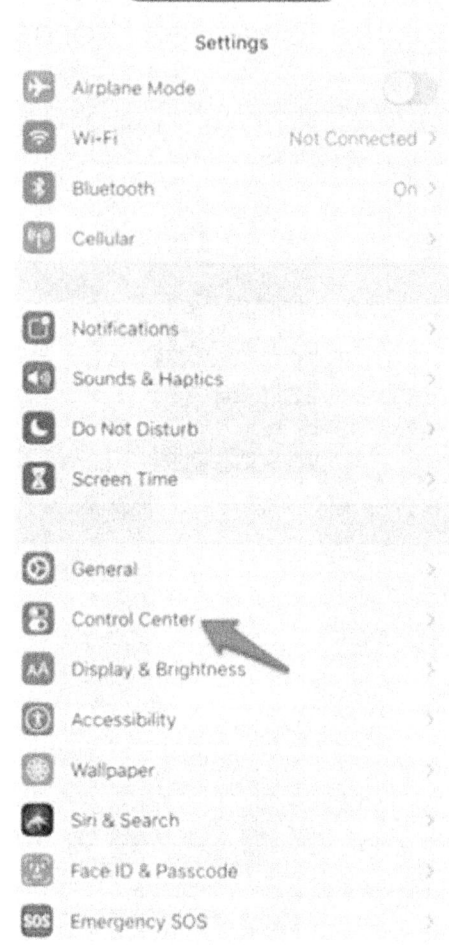

Scroll down and tap on the "green plus symbol" next to the "Dark mode icon" to add it to the "INCLUDE" section. Do this for any other button you wish to add to the Control Center.

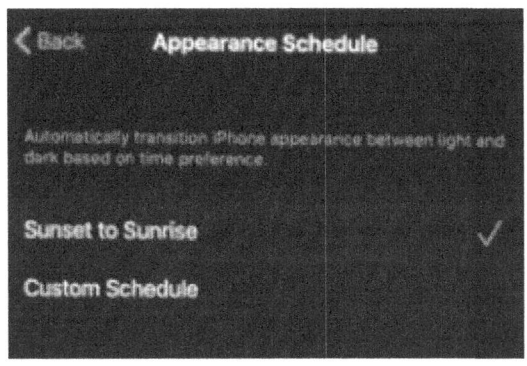

You can also schedule Dark Mode to Turn ON or OFF at a given time or period. Go to Display & Brightness > enable the "Automatic" switch > tap on "Options" > configure "Sunset to Sunrise" or select a custom schedule for light and dark mode to enable at certain times.

How to Transfer Files Between Apple Devices Using Airdrop

Airdrop is an ad-hoc network service that allows you to wirelessly transfer files over Bluetooth and Wifi between iOS devices and Macs. It could be from an iPhone to an iPad or from an iPhone to an iMac or verse versa. With Airdrop, you can send photos, videos, contacts Passbook Passes, Voice Memos, Map Locations, and everything else that appears on a share sheet between an iPhone and an iPad. When using Airdrop between two Macs, you can share virtually any file. There is no file size or type restrictions.

✓Place your iPhone 11 next to the iPad. Ensure Wi-fi and Bluetooth are turned ON on both devices in the control center.

✓Tap AirDrop icon in the control center and set it to "Everyone" to share with everyone or "Contacts Only Mode" to share with only people in your contact. The same process goes for the iPad.

✓ Go to the iPad and find a file you intend to send and tap on it (e.g, a document)

✓Tap ellipsis (...) on the upper right and click on the share option to access the share sheet. Tap on the device you wish to send the file to in the share sheet and the file is automatically sent.

If you are using AirDrop on your Mac for the first time, you may need to adjust the settings on your Mac. To do this;

✓ Open finder and choose AirDrop in the left-hand column. The settings are in blue where it says "Allow me to be discovered by". Click on the little down arrow at the end of the statement and you will be presented with similar options to what is on iOS. (No one, Contacts Only, Everyone).

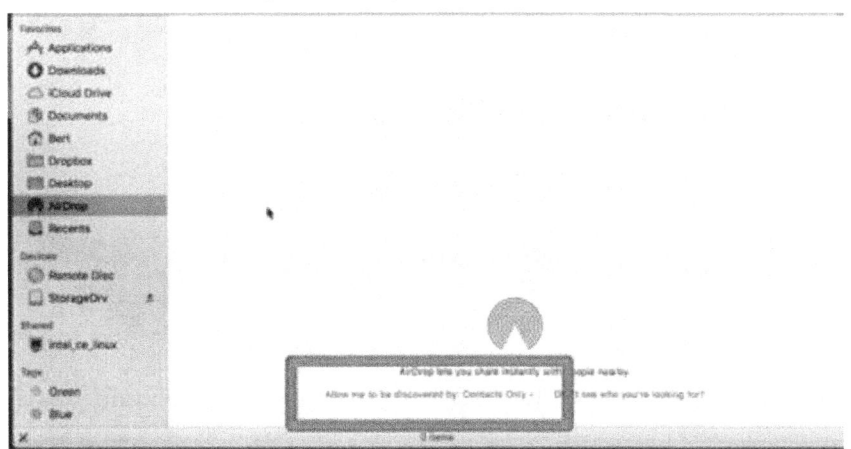

✓With this setup, you can send files between the Mac and any other iOS device.

✓Right-click or Ctrl-Click on the file you want to AirDrop, scroll to Share and click on Air Drop.

✓The AirDrop window that pops up may take time to populate. Once the person you want to send the file to pops up, simply click on them and the file is sent.

Control Center Scan QR Code Shortcut

You will find a control center QR code shortcut by:

✓ Going to settings

✓ Tap on Control Center

✓ Tap on "Customize Controls" Scroll up from the list and tap on "Scan QR Code" and QR Code shortcut will appear within the control center.

✓ Invoke the Control Center by going to the home screen

✓ Swipe down from the top right of the screen and you will find the Scan QR Code shortcut within the control center.

✓ Tap on it and it would take you to the camera app, this allows you to scan QR codes.

How to Control Your Device with Voice

Voice control features on the iPhone 11 allow you to control every aspect of your device by voice. However, it should not be confused with Siri. Voice Control is a super powerful accessibility feature for visually impaired users. Below are some voice control commands to help a visually impaired iPhone 11 user navigate through the phone with ease.

- To Open an App - Say "Open <app name>"
- To open the control center – say "Open Control Center."

- To go to the Home Screen of the iPhone – Say "Go home."
- To go one step back – say "Go back"
- To put the phone to sleep – say "Go to sleep" To interact with screen items, we use the following voice commands
- "Show grid" – the grid feature numbers the entire phone's screen with precision and each grid areas can be micro-managed by saying the number that pertains to the area of the screen.
- "Swipe left."
- "Swipe right."
- "Long press <item name>."
- "Tap <number>"
- "Turn Voice Control On."

How to Use the New Gestures for Select text, Copy, Cut, Paste, Redo and undo

You can select text, copy, cut, paste, redo and undo and event on the iPhone 11 series using gestures. To select a text area, double-tap and swipe across the text area to be selected. You can multi-select text by tapping with two fingers and drag across the text area. To copy text, highlight the text area, and pinch the text area with three fingers. Double pinch-in with three-finger gesture cuts the highlighted text area, and three fingers pinch-out paste a copied or cut text. Three fingers swipe to the left undo the previous action, and three fingers swipe to the right redo a previously undone action.

How to Use Intelligent Selection

The iPhone 11 series powered by iOS 13.1 comes with an intelligent selection feature. The intelligent selection allows you to select address, phone numbers, email address, etc without having to select an entire text area. Double-tap on an address, phone number or email address to select only the tapped item.

How to Use Cycle Tracking in Health

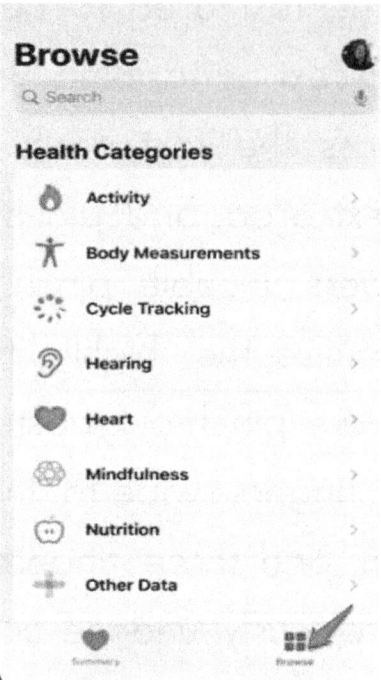

With Cycle Tracking on the iPhone, you can log in information about your menstrual cycle and get alert about your period. To get started with Cycle Tracking on your iPhone 11, open the health app > tap browse at the bottom of the screen

Select "Cycle Tracking" from the list of Health Categories > tap "Get Started" under Set up Cycle Tracking > tap "Next" to enter some details like the date of your last period. Note: Any information you enter into Cycle Tracking is encrypted when your phone is locked with a passcode, touch ID, or face ID. You can also decide which information is placed in the Health Apps and which apps can access your data via the health app. You can log a period and associated symptoms in a few steps - Open Cycle Tracking in the Health App > Tap Period > Specify your flow level.

Today, August 8

PERIOD	
Had Flow	✓
No Flow	○
FLOW LEVEL	
Light	○
Medium	✓
Heavy	○

Swipe left and log in any symptoms you are experiencing, then tap any that applies to you.

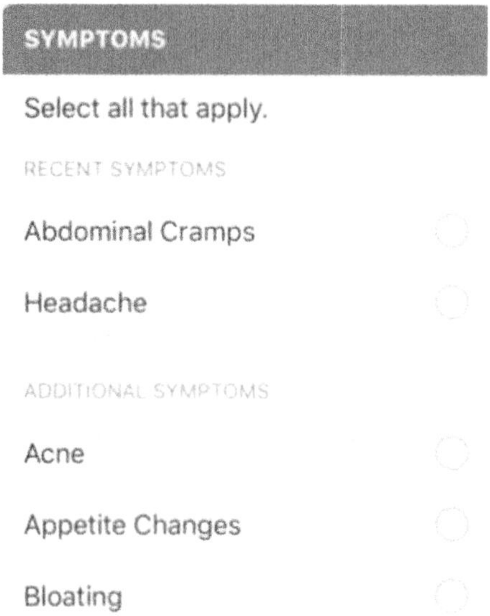

Select all that apply.

RECENT SYMPTOMS

Abdominal Cramps

Headache

ADDITIONAL SYMPTOMS

Acne

Appetite Changes

Bloating

New symptoms appear at the top of the app. >
Keep swiping left to input other data like sexual
activity

SEXUAL ACTIVITY

Had Sex

PROTECTION

Used

Not Used

Or Ovulation test result.

Positive / Peak

High

Negative / Low

Indeterminate

Tap "Done" when you are done. You can also tap on items on the other data section to add more information like sporting or Basal body temperature.

Taking a closer look at your data can help you see irregularities, and what is coming up. Check the prediction section to have a heads up on your next period or fertile window period. Below that, you find a visualization of your cycle history under Cycle History.

Current Cycle: Started Aug 6 (2 days)
3-day period

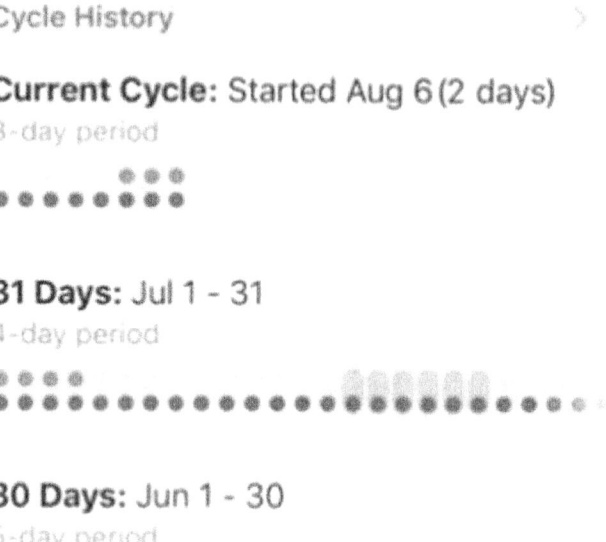

31 Days: Jul 1 - 31
4-day period

30 Days: Jun 1 - 30
5-day period

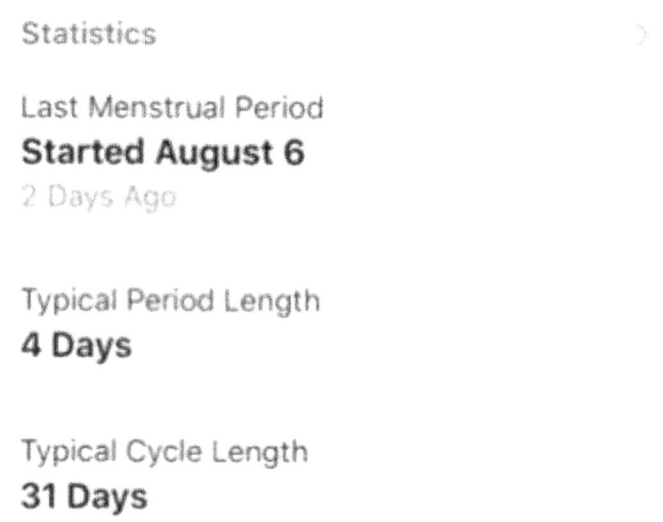

Data about your cycle is displayed under Statistics.

Statistics 〉

Last Menstrual Period
Started August 6
2 Days Ago

Typical Period Length
4 Days

Typical Cycle Length
31 Days

How to Update iOS on the iPhone

To download and install an update, Go to Settings > General > tap Software Update. You need a Wi-Fi connection to install any available update.

How to Receive Calls on Other Devices

You can decide to pick calls meant for your iPhone 11 on your other Apple devices such as your Mac or iPad logged in on your iCloud Account. To enable this, go to Settings > tap on "Phone" > choose "Call on Other Devices > Toggle ON "Allow Calls on Other Devices" > Under the "Allow Calls ON," toggle ON which device(s) you like to receive phone calls on.

You can do same for messages; go to Settings > tap on "Messages" > tap on "Text Message Forwarding" > toggle on devices you like to receive or send text messages from.

How to Configure Filming Speed On the iPhone

Whether you are a fan of shooting videos with that smooth 60 frames per second motion at 1080p or the super smooth 24 frames per second at 4K, the iPhone 11 has your back. To configure your filming speed, go to "Settings" > tap "Camera" > Select "Record Video" and choose from the list of filming speeds.

How to Recover a Stolen iPhone

You can search for a lost or stolen iPhone with the aid of the "Find my iPhone" feature on your device. If you don't have this App on your iPhone, you can download and install it. There is a new technology with iOS 13 at the background of the iPhone 11 that helps you locate your device even better. If you have Bluetooth ON on the missing phone, it relays its location through any nearby Apple device even if it is switched OFF. For instance, if the iPhone was misplaced or taken to another country and someone walks in with an iPhone or Apple device, the stolen or missing iPhone relays its current location through the other iPhone or Apple Device securely and anonymously back to Apple and then to you. You can also find a friend's missing iPhone through your iCloud Account. To turn ON the "Find my iPhone" feature;

• Go to "Settings"

• Scroll down and tap on "iCloud."

• Locate the "Find My iPad" feature and toggle it ON.

If your device gets lost or stolen, here are the steps to recover it using iCloud;

• Visit iCloud.com on a PC

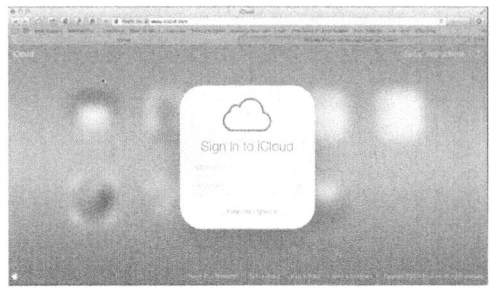

- log into your iCloud Account

- Click on the "Find My iPhone" icon.

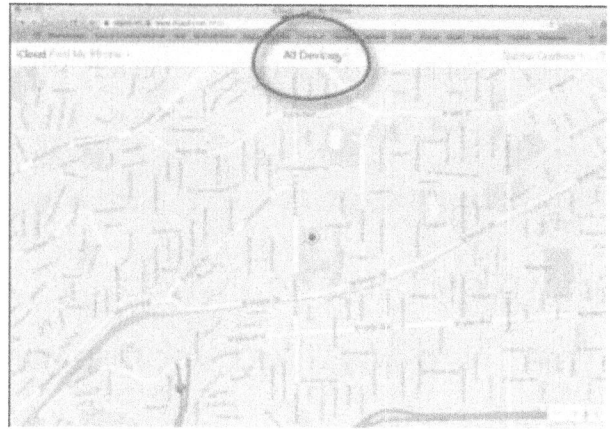

- At the top of the screen, you will find a drop down Menu with the tag "All Devices", tap on it to see all of the devices that are registered to your iCloud account and tap the device you wish to find.

- Choose the iPhone XI from the list of devices to be located.

188

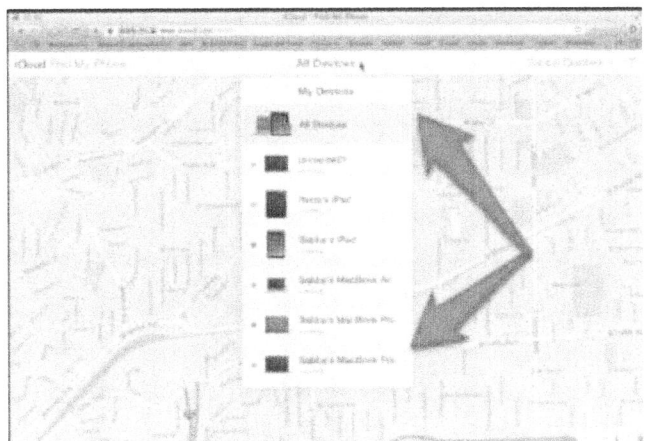

- The green button on the map indicates the exact location of the missing iPhone.

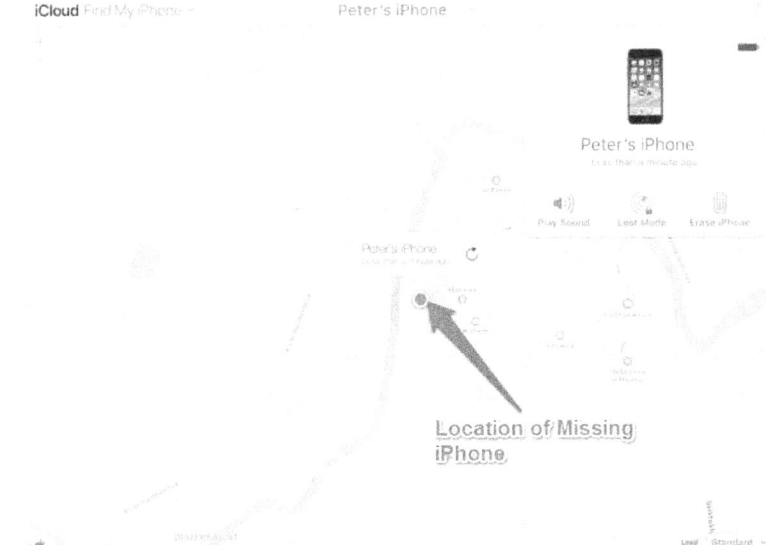

- Zoom-in as much as you want on the location to see the exact location of the device.
- If it is within the house and wasn't stolen but misplaced, Click on the "Play Sound" button.

This will activate a sound on the device so you can locate it.

Smith's iPhone 11

Offline

Notify me when found

Play Sound   Lost Mode   Erase iPhone

Remove from Account

- If you cannot locate the device because it is not connected to Wifi, Click on "Lost mode" or choose to "Erase iPhone" ensuring that no one else has access to your files or wallet. If you backed up your device before it got stolen or missing, it would be restored in your new device when you sync it to your iCloud.

- When you click on "Lost Mode" you will be requested to enter a phone number where you can be reached. This number will be shown on your missing iPhone If you don't have a passcode setup on the iPhone before it got missing; you will be requested to enter a passcode to lock the iPhone.

- After keying in the phone number, click "Next" to take you to a message box where you are to enter a message that will be shown with your phone number on your stolen or missing iPhone. The default message is "This iPhone has been lost, Please Call me." You can change it to whatever message you prefer. Unless the passcode is known, the iPhone is useless to anyone who has it. Click on "Done" when you are done typing the message.

- If you don't like the map, you can change it to standard, satellite or Hybrid mode at the bottom left side of the screen.

Made in the USA
Monee, IL
05 December 2019

18031183R00115